WESTMAR COLLEGE ✧ W9-BQY-996

The Wideness
of God's Mercy

VOLUME ONE

THE WIDENESS OF GOD'S MERCY

Litanies to Enlarge Our Prayer

Volume One

Prayers for the Church

An Ecumenical Collection Compiled and Adapted by

JEFFERY W. ROWTHORN

106944

The Seabury Press

Copyright © 1985 by Jeffery W. Rowthorn
All rights reserved. No part of this book may be reproduced, stored in a retrieval system, or transmitted, in any form or by any means, electronic, mechanical, photocopying, recording, or otherwise, without the written permission of Winston Press, Inc.

Library of Congress Catalog Card Number: 84-52316

ISBN: 0-86683-789-2 (two-volume set)
ISBN: 0-86683-794-9 (Volume One)
ISBN: 0-86683-795-7 (Volume Two)

Printed in the United States of America

5 4 3 2 1

Winston Press, Inc.
430 Oak Grove
Minneapolis, Minnesota

For Anne

    Virginia, Christian and Peregrine

  —their love

    has enlarged my life;

    their lives

    have enlarged my prayer.

Contents

PRAYER AND WORSHIP

Intercession: Ancient and Modern

Adoration and Praise

PRAYER AND TIME

Saints and Commemorations

Dedications and Anniversaries

PRAYER AND THE CHURCH

Its Unity

Its Sacraments

Its Ministry

Acknowledgments

For permission to reprint material in these volumes, grateful acknowledgment is made to the individuals and publishers named on the pages below:

Abingdon Press for selections from *Lift Up Your Hearts* by Walter Russell Bowie. Copyright renewal © 1976 by Walter Russell Bowie. Used by permission of the publishers, Abingdon Press.

George Allen and Unwin for "The Southwell Litany" by Bishop G. Ridding of Southwell.

Horace T. Allen, Jr. for his "Litany of Dedication."

Allyn and Bacon, Inc., for selections from *The Student Prayer Book* by J. Oliver Nelson, copyright © 1953 by Haddam House, Inc. Edited and written by a Haddam House Committee under the chairmanship of John Oliver Nelson, Association Press, New York, 1953.

American Bible Society for Scripture quotations designated GNB from the *Good News Bible*, the Bible in Today's English Version. Copyright © 1976 by the American Bible Society.

Andrews, McMeel & Parker Inc. for an excerpt from *Prayers from the Burned-Out City* by Robert W. Castle, Jr. Copyright 1968 by Sheed & Ward, Inc. Reprinted with permission of Andrews, McMeel & Parker Inc. All rights reserved.

Ascension Lutheran Church, Baltimore, Maryland, and the Lutheran Church in America, for a litany from *Monday's Ministries: The Ministry of the Laity* by Melvin Vos; edited by Raymond Tiemeyer, Parish Life Press, Philadelphia, 1979.

Augsburg Publishing House for selections reprinted from *Lutheran Book of Worship*, copyright © 1978, by permission of Augsburg Publishing House; for material reprinted by permission from *Table Prayers* by Mildred Tengbom, copyright © 1977 Augsburg Publishing House.

Ave Maria Press for material excerpted from *Praise Him!* edited by William G. Storey. Copyright © 1973 by Ave Maria Press, Notre Dame, IN 46556. Used with permission of the publisher.

The Rev. Martha Blacklock for "The God of Our Mothers."

Bloch Publishing Company for "Litany for Days of Penitence" from *The Authorized Daily Prayer Book, Revised Edition*, by Joseph H. Hertz, Bloch Publishing Company, Inc., New York.

Bread for the World for litanies published for use as worship aids.

Avery Brooke for two litanies written by her and published by *St. Luke's Quarterly*, St. Luke's Parish, Darien, CT, © 1963.

Katherine Meyer Cafolla for "Confessions of the Community."

The Central Conference of American Rabbis for permission to reproduce litanies from *Gates of Prayer*. Copyright © 1975 by C.C.A.R. and U.L.P.S. Reprinted by permission.

Church Hymnal Corporation for selections from *Book of Occasional Services,* Copyright © 1979 by The Church Pension Fund. Used by permission of The Church Pension Fund.

Church of the Province of South Africa, Publications Department, for selections from *The South African Liturgy 1975*. Used by permission.

Collins Publishers, London, for an excerpt adapted from *Prayers for Help and Healing* by William Barclay.

Concordia Publishing House for selections from *Help it All Make Sense, Lord*. Copyright © 1972 by Concordia Publishing House. Used by permission; and for selections from *Time to Pray: Daily Prayers for Youth*, © 1960 Concordia Publishing House. Used by permission.

The Confraternity of Christian Doctrine, Inc. for "Canticle of the Blessed Virgin Mary," Luke 1. 46-55 taken from the *New American Bible*. Copyright © 1970 by the Confraternity of Christian Doctrine, Washington, D.C. Used with permission.

C.S.S. Publishing Co. for selections from *Contemporary Altar Prayers, Volume 3* by Larry Hard. Material slightly altered.

J.M. Dent, Ltd., London, for selections from *Devotional Services for Public Worship*, 1903.

Diocese of Brooklyn Liturgical Commission for excerpts from "The Litany for the Breaking of Bread" from the *125th Anniversary Mass* composed by the Reverend Joseph Roff in 1978.

Wm. B. Eerdmans Publishing Company for selections from *Contemporary Prayers for Public Worship*, edited by Caryl Micklem. Used by permission.

Epworth Press, London, for selections from *John Wesley's Prayers*, edited by F.C. Gill.

Eyre & Spottiswoode Ltd. for extracts from the Silver Jubilee Service and the Royal Maundy Service, which are copyright, and extracts from *The Book of Common Prayer*, which is Crown Copyright. Included with permission.

Fides/Claretian for selections from *Prayers in Community* by T. Maertens and M. De Bilde, translated by J. Ducharme, and *Pray Like This: Materials for the Practice of Dynamic Group Prayer* by W. G. Storey.

Fortress Press for selections from *Prayers for Public Worship* by Carl T. Uehling. Copyright © 1972 by Fortress Press. Adapted with the permission of the author and Fortress Press; and for selections from *Interrobang* by N. C. Habel. Copyright © 1969 by Fortress Press. Altered and used by permission of Fortress Press.

Galaxy Music Corporation for words of the hymn "God of Concrete, God of Steel" from *Worship for Today*, edited by Richard G. Jones. The words "God of Concrete, God of Steel" copyright © 1968 by Richard G. Jones used by permission of Galaxy Music Corporation, New York, New York, sole U.S. agent.

The General Synod of the Church of England for the Ten Commandments and our Lord's Summary of the Law which are reproduced in a slightly adapted form from the Order for Holy Communion Rite A in *The Alternative Service Book 1980* (Church of England) with permission.

Ernest Gordon for excerpts from the order of service of the Princeton University Chapel. Used with permision.

The Grail, England, for Psalm 136, slightly adapted, from *The Psalms: A New Translation* published by William Collins, Sons & Co Ltd. and the Paulist Press.

The Reverend Canon Charles Mortimer Guilbert, S.T.D., for material from *Prayers, Thanksgivings, and Litanies*, © 1973 by Charles Mortimer Guilbert as Custodian of the *Standard Book of Common Prayer*.

Harper & Row, Publishers, Inc., for excerpt from *Prayers for Daily Use* by Samuel H. Miller, copyright © 1957 by Samuel H. Miller;
for adaptation of "A Litany of Praise," "A Litany of the Tongue," "A Litany of Friendship," "A Litany of the Home," "A New Year's Litany," and "The Dedication of an Organ" from *A Book of Public Prayers* by Harry Emerson Fosdick, copyright © 1959 by Harry Emerson Fosdick;

and for adaptation of "A Thanksgiving for Hospitals" from *Prayers for Help and Healing* by William Barclay, copyright © 1968 by William Barclay. All reprinted by permission of Harper & Row, Publishers, Inc.

Hinshaw Music, Inc., for the hymn "Earth's Scattered Isles and Contoured Hills," copyright © 1977 by Hinshaw Music, Inc. Used by permission August 22, 1984.

Hope Publishing Comany for the hymn "When in Our Music God Is Glorified," copyright © 1972 by Hope Publishing Co., Carol Stream, IL 60187. All Rights Reserved. Used by Permission.

Hymns Ancient and Modern, Ltd. for "Lift High the Cross." Reprinted by permission of Hymns Ancient & Modern, Ltd.

International Committee on English in the Liturgy, Inc., (ICEL) for excerpts from the English translation of the Roman Missal. Copyright © 1973, International Committee on English in the Liturgy, Inc. All rights reserved.

Richard G. Jones for selection from *Worship for Today: Suggestions and Ideas*, edited by Richard G. Jones.

The Liturgical Conference for litany from *The Book of Catholic Worship*. © The Liturgical Conference, 810 Rhode Island Ave., N.E., Washington, D.C. 20018. All rights reserved. Used with permission;
and for material from *Liturgy Magazine*.

The Liturgical Press for selections from *Scripture Services* by John Gallen, S.J. Published by The Liturgical Press. Copyrighted by The Order of St. Benedict, Inc., Collegeville, Minnesota, 1963.

Longman Group Limited for extracts from *Early Christian Prayers*, edited by A. Hamman, O.F.M. English translation by Walter Mitchell. Copyright © 1961 by Longman Group Limited, London.

The Memorial Church, Harvard University, for the prayer "The Search for Truth" by Willard Sperry, published in *With One Voice—Prayers from around the World* (Thomas Y. Crowell Co., New York, 1961).

Methodist Publishing House, London, for selection from *Methodist Book of Offices 1936*.

Methuen & Co. Ltd. for selections from *Preces Privatae of Lancelot Andrewes, Bishop of Winchester*, edited by A.E. Burn.

Morehouse-Barlow Co., Inc., for selections from *The Covenant of Peace: A Liberation Prayer Book*, edited by John P. Brown and Richard York. Used by permission of Morehouse-Barlow Co., Inc.

A. R. Mowbray and Co., Ltd., for selections from *Intercessions at Holy Communion on Themes for the Church Year* by Raymond Hockley; for selections from the Taizé Office, translated by Anthony Brown, copyright © 1966 by Mowbrays Publishing Division; from a *Priest's Book of Private Devotion*; and for a selection from *A Nation at Prayer* by W. B. Trevelyan, as published in *Prayers for a New World*, compiled by J. W. Suter, Scribner's, New York, 1964.

Nashdom Abbey in Burnham, Slough, U.K., for "The Litany of Jesus Praying" in a slightly adapted form.

New Century Publishers, Inc., for material reprinted from *Treat Me Cool, Lord*. Copyright © 1968 by Carl F. Burke. By permission of New Century Publishers, Inc., Piscataway, N.J. 08854.

Ursula M. Niebuhr for "For All Workers," a prayer written by Reinhold Niebuhr and originally published in *Hymns for Worship*, prepared for the Student Christian Movement and published by Association Press in 1939.

Oxford University Press for selections from *Spilled Milk: Litanies for Living* by Kay Smallzried; for selections from *Praise God: Common Prayer at Taizé*, translated by E. Chisholm. Copyright © 1975; for selections from *The Kingdom, The Power, and The Glory: Services of Praise and Prayer for Occasional Use in Churches* (American edition of the Grey Book). Copyright © 1933 by Oxford University Press, New York; for litanies from *The Cuddesdon Office Book;* for litanies from *The Book of Common Worship of The Church of South India*; for the hymn "Lord, Save Your World" by Albert Bayly.

Paulist Press for selection from *Service Resources for Pastoral Ministry*, 1976, #1. Used by permission of Paulist Press.

Laurence Pollinger Limited for "Grace Before Meals" from *Prayers for Daily Use* by Samuel H. Miller.

Pueblo Publishing Co. for excerpt from *Prayers of the Faithful: Cycles A, B, C*. Copyright © 1977 by Pueblo Publishing Company, Inc. Used by permission of Pueblo Publishing Company, Inc.

Random House, Inc. for an excerpt from "For the Time Being: A Christmas Oratorio," from *W. H. Auden: Collected Poems*, edited by Edward Mendelson, © 1946 by Random House.

Resource Publications for "Dayyenu: It Would Have Been Enough," by Michael E. Moynahan, S.J. Reprinted with permisson from *Modern Liturgy*, a creative resource journal for worship and the liturgical arts, P.O. Box 444, Saratoga, CA 95071.

SCM Press for selections from *Contemporary Prayers for Public Worship*, edited by Caryl Micklem, SCM Press, 1967;
from *Epilogues and Prayers* by William Barclay, SCM Press, 1963;
and from *Prayers for the Christian Year* by William Barclay, SCM Press, 1964.

Charles Scribner's Sons for adaptation from Twelfth, Eighteenth, and Twenty-fifth Day prayers and adaptation from Thirtieth Day Prayer, here entitled "St. Paul," from *A Diary of Private Prayer* by John Baillie. Copyright © 1949 by Charles Scribner's Sons; copyright renewed 1977 by Ian Fowler Baillie. Reprinted with the permission of Charles Scribner's Sons.

The Seabury Press for selections from *A Book of Family Prayer* by Gabe Huck. Copyright © 1979 by the Seabury Press, Inc. Used by permission.

The Society for Promoting Christian Knowledge for "A Litany of Intercession for the Diocese" with minor changes from *Ember Prayers: A Collection of Prayers for the Ministry of the Church*, compiled by John Neale, SPCK, London, 1965;
for material from *Acts of Devotion*, SPCK, London, 1928;
and for material from *The Daily Office Revised*, © The Joint Liturgical Group, 1978, reproduced by permission of SPCK.

Sojourners Fellowship, 1309 L Street N.W., Washington, DC 20005, for material first used by the Sojourners Fellowship or published in *Sojourners*.

Abbot Jerome Theisen, O.S.B., St. John's Abbey, Collegeville, Minnesota, for "The Mystery of the Cross."

Keith Watkins for the litany "God of the Coming Age."

Herbert B. West for the litany "With People at Work" from his book of prayers entitled *Stay Wth Me, Lord: A Man's Prayers*, Seabury Press, New York, 1974.

The Westminster Press for selections used and revised from *The Worshipbook — Services and Hymns*. Copyright © MCMLXX, MCMLXXII, The Westminster Press. Revised and used by permission.

Rev. R. H. L. Williams for material from *Prayers for Today's Church* (Falcon Books, London, 1972, and Augsburg, Minneapolis, 1977).

World Council of Churches for a litany from *A Suggested Use for Pentecost, Christian Unity Sunday* entitled "An Act of Intercession for the Whole Church of Christ."

World Library Publications, Inc., for eight litanies from *Come, Lord Jesus*, © 1976, 1981 by Lucien Deiss. Reprinted with permission. Unlawful to reproduce in any way any of the copyrighted material contained in this book.

Worldview for portions of "Appeal for Theological Affirmation," the so-called Hartford Appeal, published in *Worldview*, April 1975.

Yale Divinity School for "The Prayers of Adoration, Confession, and Thanksgiving," from *Laudamus: Services and Songs of Praise*.

Preface

Since the Introduction which follows is meant to address the issues of how, when and where, liturgically speaking, the litanies in this collection may be used, this Preface can be devoted entirely to expressions of gratitude to those who have helped to bring this book to completion.

In the first place, I am grateful to The Seabury Press and to Avery Brooke, its Publisher, for the invitation to compile an extensive ecumenical collection of litanies. My editors, Jack Whelan of the Seabury Press and more recently Hermann Weinlick of Winston Press, are to be thanked for their great patience in waiting, and their good counsel in advising, as the book has moved slowly towards its goal.

I much appreciate the sabbatical leave which Yale and Berkeley Divinity Schools granted me in the second semester of the 1980–1981 academic year. During that leave this book had its beginnings in the relaxing and hospitable environment of St. John's Abbey and University in Collegeville, Minnesota. To the Institute for Ecumenical and Cultural Research and Dr. Robert Bilheimer, its Executive Director, and to the Benedictines of St. John's and Abbot Jerome Theisen, O.S.B., go my heartfelt thanks for a memorable winter and spring in their company. I am also grateful to those good friends who were Fellows at the Institute with me; they encouraged me in this endeavor and generously helped me to reflect on the purpose and place of litanies in the public prayer of the Church.

I gathered much of my material at two libraries: the Alcuin Library at St. John's and the Library of Luther-Northwestern Seminary in St. Paul, Minnesota. To the staff of these libraries I want to express my appreciation for a warm welcome and ready collaboration.

The book continued on its way after my return to New Haven, and I am conscious of the great debt I owe to Victoria Strane who typed every word of every litany and, with a rare enthusiasm, offered invaluable comments and suggestions. If all of the faults of this book are of my making, some of its virtues are surely due to her.

The book came to an end at St. Saviour's Episcopal Church in Bar Harbor, Maine, where I was made most welcome in July 1982 as the summer supply priest in the absence on vacation of the Rector, the Rev. Michael Dugan. Bar Harbor was as congenial a place to end this project as Collegeville was to begin it.

I am also grateful to the Rev. Arthur Underwood, Episcopal Chaplain to Yale University, and to Dr. Jon Bailey, Director of the Yale Institute of Sacred Music, for use of office facilities during the time when the manuscript was being typed.

I would like to acknowledge with gratitude the willingness of the various owners of copyrighted material to allow many of these litanies to appear here, often in a form markedly different from the original, for reasons to be made plain in the Introduction. Every effort has been made to locate the copyright holders. If any errors or omissions have been made, they should be brought to the attention of the publishers and will be gladly corrected in any subsequent edition of this book.

Finally, I thank my family for living with this project while it was being begun, continued and ended. I appreciate their patience and encouragement but, as the dedication of this volume indicates, I value their love and their lives still more.

These litanies have been compiled and adapted in the hope that they will indeed enlarge the prayer of all who pray them, and I now offer them to the Church with the prayer that I have tried to pray faithfully over many years:

> Go before us, O Lord, in all our doings with thy most gracious favor, and further us now with thy continual help, that in all our works, begun, continued, and ended in thee, we may glorify thy holy Name; through Christ our Lord. Amen.

Yale and Berkeley Divinity Schools
New Haven, Connecticut   March 21, 1985

Introduction

Liturgy is the work of the whole people of God, in praise and prayer. Christ,
our High Priest and heavenly Intercessor, has made us "a kingdom, priests to
his God and Father" (Revelation 1:6). The Father's family, taken as a whole, is
"a holy priesthood, to offer spiritual sacrifices acceptable to God through
Jesus Christ" (I Peter 2:5). Moreover, it is a characteristic of Christian worship
that all should participate effectively in the liturgy.[1]

These words from Brother Max Thurian's introduction to *Eucharist at Taizé*
define the nature of all liturgical prayer undertaken by groups of Christians
assembled for worship. They also provide the proper context for evaluating
and using this collection of litanies.

Since its inception the Taizé community, originally Protestant and now
impressively ecumenical, has sought to renew its life in the world (and the
lives of those who worship with the brothers) "by means of the best possible
participation in liturgical worship."[2] This book aims at much the same goal.
It seeks to bring about the best possible participation in one essential
element of corporate worship – prayer for others as well as for oneself,
prayer for the world as well as for the Church.

Needless to say, prayer of this kind "for all sorts and conditions of men,"[3]
for humanity in all its needs and aspects, will only be undertaken more
faithfully, more frequently and more fervently in our day if it is inspired and
filled by Christ himself. The effectiveness of these litanies depends, as all
prayer must, on the Spirit of Christ who "comes to the aid of our
weakness." For, as St. Paul goes on to say, "we do not even know how we
ought to pray, but through our inarticulate groans the Spirit himself is
pleading for us."[4] Many of these litanies may indeed appear to be not in the
least inarticulate, yet they will not express the faith or fuel the witness of any
Christian community unless they are one dimension of that sacrificial
worship which Paul speaks of elsewhere in Romans:

1

Therefore, my brothers and sisters, I implore you by God's mercy to offer your very selves to him: a living sacrifice, dedicated and fit for God's acceptance, the worship offered by mind and heart.[5]

However, if they are a faithful embodiment of that "worship offered by mind and heart," then they will truly become the effective prayer of the people of God.

The contemporary rediscovery of the "Prayers of the People," as they are appropriately called, is one facet of the liturgical renewal which in the past half-century has increasingly reshaped the worship of much of the Church. Intercessory prayer is once again understood and commended as a priestly ministry which God entrusts to the entire company of the faithful. By virtue of our baptism, we all enjoy this high calling to pray for the world and for people everywhere. Novel as this claim may seem to some people, it is – like many liturgical developments in this present age – simply the reappropriation of something genuinely primitive in the life of the Christian community.

In the middle years of the first century St. Paul wrote:

First of all, then, I urge that petitions, prayers, intercessions, and thanksgivings be offered for all people; for sovereigns and all in high office, that we may lead a tranquil and quiet life in full observance of religion and high standards of morality.[6]

Episcopalians and others will have heard a clear echo of this apostolic injunction Sunday by Sunday in the opening phrases of Cranmer's *Prayer for the Whole State of Christ's Church* (see Litany 5):

Almighty and everliving God who by thy holy Apostle hast taught us to make prayers, and supplications, and to give thanks for all men; We humbly beseech thee most mercifully . . . to receive these our prayers, which we offer unto thy Divine Majesty.

In the second century, in his brief description of Sunday worship, Justin Martyr records that the assembled company offered up prayers "for all people everywhere."[7] However, the scope and content of these prayers only become known to us in the classical liturgies of the fourth century and in such innovations as the Kyrie litany of Pope Gelasius a century later (Litany 13). Here the range of concern is wide indeed, not least because the Church's domain had also widened until in places it was co-terminous with society at large.

Paul's desire that in every place holy hands should be lifted in prayer[8] led in time to the emergence of litanies as the principal vehicle of the people's corporate ministry of intercession. Four things can be said of this early form of prayer:

2

(i)	it was broad in scope, far transcending the immediate needs or narrow interests of those who were praying;
(ii)	it was as highly regarded as the *Eighteen Benedictions* (Litany 12), which had come to be referred to among Jews, quite simply, as *Tefillah* – *The* Prayer;
(iii)	it was regular, forming an integral part of the Sunday liturgy; and
(iv)	it was participatory, both in posture ("holy hands lifted in prayer") and in the repeated use of a familiar response after each petition (*Kyrie eleison* or *Amen.*)

Consequently, for a period, at least, in Christian history "intercessory prayer" and "litany" were virtually synonymous.

In the Western Church the intercessions were eventually placed within the Canon or Eucharistic Prayer. Although this was regarded as a place of honor, at the very heart of the Mass, the fact that the Canon came to be recited inaudibly meant that, to all intents and purposes, there were no longer any "Prayers of the People." In the Church's principal act of worship Sunday by Sunday an essential element was now lacking. Only the Solemn Prayers recited on Good Friday (Litany 69) and the Litany of the Saints (Litany 90), together with certain penitential litanies, survived as reminders of an earlier and universal liturgical practice.

During the later Middle Ages attempts were made to compensate for this loss. Biddings were introduced which made it possible to call on the people to pray for matters of immediate concern and local interest (Litany 2). Then in 1544, with the approval of King Henry VIII, Thomas Cranmer took the momentous step of issuing the *Great Litany* in English (Litany 1). Now the whole of the people's life could be lifted up in the people's prayer in the people's own language. For that reason the *Great Litany* is given the place of honor in this collection. It also has the distinction of being the very first service in English to have received official authorization for use throughout the Church of England.

In the various churches of the Reformation little provision was made for the "Prayers of the People." Generally they were usurped by a lengthy pastoral prayer recited by the minister without any interpolations or even responses on the part of the people. Even the *Prayer for the Whole State of Christ's Church* in the Anglican liturgy allowed for no variation or application to the present moment, and the people's participation was limited to the final Amen. Neither in Roman Catholic nor in Protestant congregations were the laity able to exercise the priestly ministry of intercession which was theirs by virtue of their baptism. The apostolic injunction in I Timothy languished for reasons of benign neglect. The urgency, sensitivity and sustained attention which intercessory prayer clearly calls for on the congregation's part were for centuries far more the exception than the rule in public worship.

Since the middle years of this century a process of change, startling in its cumulative effect, has been under way. One clear indication of this is the recent statement, *Baptism, Eucharist and Ministry*, issued by the Faith and Order Commission of the World Council of Churches.[9] Under the auspices of the Commission more than a hundred theologians met in Lima, Peru, in January 1982. They represented "virtually all the major church traditions: Eastern Orthodox, Oriental Orthodox, Roman Catholic, Old Catholic, Lutheran, Anglican, Reformed, Methodist, United, Disciples, Baptist, Adventist and Pentecostal."[10] In their agreed statement, transmitted by unanimous vote "for the common study and official response of the churches," they made this affirmation:

> The world, to which renewal is promised, is present in the whole eucharistic celebration. The world is present in the thanksgiving to the Father, where the Church speaks on behalf of the whole creation; in the memorial of Christ, where the Church, united with its great High Priest and Intercessor, prays for the world; in the prayer for the gift of the Holy Spirit, where the Church asks for sanctification and new creation.[11]

Furthermore, it is the calling of every Christian community and person "to identify with the joys and sufferings of all people as they seek to witness [to Christ and to their faith in his coming kingdom] in caring love."[12]

This caring love which is spoken of here has as one of its elements, and indeed as its necessary prelude and constant companion, the willingness to pray for all people and all of life. This in itself is a dimension of loving one's neighbor as oneself and of respecting "the dignity of every human being."[13] Consequently, the Second Vatican Council made provision for the restoration of "the common prayer" or "the prayer of the faithful," which now, as in the early Church, is to follow the Gospel reading and the homily:

> By this prayer, in which the people are to take part, intercession will be made for holy Church, for the civil authorities, for those oppressed by various needs, for all mankind, and for the salvation of the entire world.[14]

The General Instruction of the Roman Missal indicates that "in special celebrations, such as confirmations, marriages, funerals, etc., the list of intentions may be more closely concerned with the special occasion."[15] Thus, at every Mass celebrated with a congregation, "the people exercise their priestly function by interceding for all mankind." This is to take the form either of a common response after each intention or of silent prayer together. It is hardly surprising, therefore, that, to achieve this end, the litany has been recovered as a primary vehicle for the "Prayers of the People."

4

This collection of litanies is intended to contribute to the restoration of the local congregation's calling to pray for the world. Both its title and its subtitle point to important aspects of that ministry of prayer and to deeply held convictions which have determined the contents of this book.

In the first place, the title is derived from the familiar hymn, *There's a Wideness in God's Mercy*.[16] Written by an Anglican priest who became a Roman Catholic, it is included in many Protestant hymnals and sung by many Protestant congregations. Its first stanza celebrates a truth about God which provides the incentive and impetus we need if we are to pray confidently for people everywhere:

> There's a wideness in God's mercy
> Like the wideness of the sea:
> There's a kindness in his justice
> Which is more than liberty.
> There is welcome for the sinner,
> And more graces for the good;
> There is mercy with the Savior,
> There is healing in his blood.[17]

Because God's mercy knows no limits, because "the love of God is broader than the measure of man's mind," we can cry *Kyrie eleison* in full assurance that our prayer will be heard and answered. God intends everyone to come within the reach of his saving embrace, made visible to us in Christ's arms of love outstretched on the hard wood of the cross.[18] Consequently, the range of these litanies is deliberately as broad as possible. There are some sins of omission, but it is to be hoped that leaders of prayer and planners of liturgy will find here an abundance of models and patterns which will be of use in preparing litanies for occasions and topics which are overlooked in this collection. As the earliest prayer known to us outside the New Testament (Litany 14) demonstrates, ours must be a prayer for all needs. No one book can do more than begin to formulate the words of so universal a prayer.

However, such a book as this can certainly help in this regard. It can also serve the same purpose as that (legendary?) organ fashioned by St. Cecilia, the patroness of church music. In the words of W.H. Auden, "this innocent virgin constructed an organ *to enlarge her prayer*."[19] To use a phrase beloved by the Puritans, "stinted prayer" has been a characteristic of much of our worship: stinted by clerical monopoly, by unthinking repetition, by monologue rather than dialogue, by narrow interests and limited imagination. The litanies in this collection are, on the contrary, participatory and wide-ranging, inviting congregations to stretch their praying for others beyond accustomed limits and familiar themes. As St. Paul once wrote to the Christians at Philippi,

Have no anxiety about anything, but in everything by prayer and supplication with thanksgiving let your requests be made known to God.[20]

"In everything" is a challenge to our stinted praying. We are called to grow into a life of prayer for others which is expansive enough to accommodate and nourish even the most generous Christian spirit. So often that kind of spirit is being stifled at the present time. The litanies in this book are meant to lengthen the stride and strengthen the weak knees of those who walk in the company of the High Priest who "always lives to make intercession" for us.[21] In this sense they are indeed litanies to enlarge our prayer.

The use to which these litanies are put in worship will vary from tradition to tradition. Certain of them can be employed as the "Prayers of the People," serving as the climax of the Liturgy of the Word after the Gospel has been read, preached, and affirmed. In non-eucharistic settings they can be used in place of the minister's pastoral prayer or at the close of a morning or evening office. Carefully chosen, one of the litanies could be an appropriate congregational response to a sermon preached on a particular text or theme. Some are seasonal litanies, others belong in services clearly focused on such concerns as the unity of the Church, the peace of the world, the nurture of the young, or the care of the elderly. Some are meant to be sung or said in procession; no pieces of paper would be required since the same refrain is repeated throughout the litany and thus is readily learned and used (the chief reason for the popularity of litanies in the past). In the case of litanies employing more than one voice or the successive stanzas of a hymn, careful preparation is obviously called for.

In any event, each occasion of public worship should allow for an *ample* time of common prayer for others. Without doing violence to the tradition of a particular church or the structure of a given liturgical rite, it is certainly possible to make use of the litany form of prayer week by week or from time to time. As in every other aspect of liturgical planning and leadership, pastoral sensitivity and imagination are needed if these litanies are to be grafted faithfully and with integrity into the worship of a particular community of faith.

The most helpful demonstration of how this book can be used with pastoral sensitivity and imagination is to let the litanies speak for themselves. Each of the examples cited below will indicate ways in which that particular litany and others like it may serve to enlarge the Church's prayer.

Litany 1	*Adaptability and Selectivity*
	These two principles are well illustrated in this first litany. The rubrics (instructions) indicate that it may be used in whole or in part. In addition, the leader is free to select some of the many petitions and omit others in order to shorten the litany. In the *Book of Common Prayer 1979*, from which it is taken, the rubrics also point out that it may be used in a variety of ways to suit a variety of needs and occasions: "To be said or sung, kneeling, standing, or in procession."[22]

Litany 6	*Silence*
	The restoration of the "Prayers of the People" requires that silent prayer on the part of the whole congregation be taken with great seriousness and that ample time be allowed for it between the biddings or petitions. Instruction on the creative use of silence in corporate prayer of this kind may well be needed. What matters is that neither leader nor congregation be intimidated by sustained periods of silence. Those fearful of silence will inevitably be tempted to curtail it or to fill it needlessly with yet more words.

Litany 7	*Free Intercessions*
	At three points in this litany the congregation is invited to add their own petitions and thanksgivings. Ample time is again the secret of success, together with instruction, encouragement and some attention to the question of audibility, especially in a large space or a numerous company. As in the case of silence, spontaneous contributions to a litany of this kind will increase as people become familiar and comfortable with an as yet novel form of corporate prayer.

Litany 8	*Particular Intentions*
	As an alternative to intercessions freely interpolated into an otherwise formal litany, the leader may mention at the start various people and concerns in order that the congregation may bear them in mind during the ensuing litany. This is yet another way of ensuring that a general prayer is firmly rooted in specific lives and needs.

Litany 13   *Ancient Prayers*
The *Kyrie Litany* of Pope Gelasius was first used
almost fifteen centuries ago. It has been discreetly
modernized here in order to allow so ancient a prayer
to be used in our day by people whose fundamental
needs and concerns are not markedly different from
those of their fifth-century forebears in the faith.

Litanies 15–16 *Sung Prayer*
Traditionally, litanies were meant to be sung. The
Lutheran Book of Worship provides simple settings of
both these litanies, and this draws attention to the
role of the trained church musician. In many
churches the minister of music is entirely capable of
writing musical settings for some of the litanies in
this collection. The capacities of leader, choir, and
congregation should be borne in mind, and some
time devoted to teaching the people their response(s).
Once the congregation is assured and can play a full
part in the singing of the litany, it could well be sung
in procession on an appropriate occasion.

Litany 44   *Dependence on Scripture*
This litany shows the author's imaginative and
faithful use of the New Testament. Indeed, Lucien
Deiss originally called his book *Prières Bibliques*
(Biblical Prayers). This particular litany may well
inspire others to obey the Gospel injunction: "Go and
do likewise."[23]

Litany 46   *Teaching the People their Part*
The *Godspell* setting of this nineteenth-century hymn
is familiar to a great number of people. The refrain
after each stanza could be sung by both voices first,
and then echoed each time by the congregation. On
the other hand, the congregation could join the two
leaders in singing the refrain as soon as they felt that
they had learned it. Some present would, of course,
be able to join in immediately. Either method is an
easy and effective way of teaching the people their
part in a sung litany.

Litany 78   *Controversial Content*
This litany should certainly be used but needs to be preceded by teaching or preaching which would indicate its thoroughly Biblical character. Without that preparation it may serve only to divide, and in that way people may be wrongly spared the "hard sayings" which are the rough edges of the Gospel proclaimed and lived by Jesus Christ.

Litany 83   *Hymn Stanzas as Part of a Litany*
Another effective way of helping people to sing parts of a litany is illustrated here. The tune must be familiar if congregational participation is to be strong and confident. Many such combinations are possible; for example, a litany on the different phases of the working day would be wonderfully enriched if used with Jan Struther's hymn, "Lord of all hopefulness."[24] Similarly, a litany concerned with healing could be well matched with F. Pratt Green's hymn, "O Christ, the Healer, we have come."[25] Here again the role of the minister of music is of the greatest importance in fashioning litanies for congregational use.

Litany 91   *Open-ended Prayer*
This *Invocation of the Saints* would surely prompt the participants to add their own heroes and heroines of the faith to an already impressive "cloud of witnesses." Leaders of prayer are often fearful of this, lest heresy or the instant canonization of some dubious characters should result! However, if we affirm the calling of every Christian to pray in the Spirit for the world at large, it requires a willingness on our part to trust those who "share with us in [Christ's] eternal priesthood."[26]

Litany 120   *Appropriate Leadership*
This litany calls for members of the various Christian traditions to lead it. Likewise, Litany 119 would be strikingly effective if the different voices belonged to people whose spiritual home was in the particular Christian communion mentioned in each paragraph of the prayer.

9

Litany 147   *Adapting to a Particular Tradition*
               This litany demonstrates the need for care and
               forethought in using material which clearly derives
               from and speaks to a particular tradition or
               denomination. New ministers are installed in
               churches of every tradition. As a result this litany,
               like others in this collection, can be imaginatively
               adapted to the needs of other traditions and
               situations. They cannot be taken over uncritically, nor
               need they be abandoned because at first glance they
               seem to belong elsewhere in the Christian household!

Litany 148   *Long Litanies*
               This is a very lengthy litany which could certainly be
               used in a shortened form. However, there is much to
               be said for using it only when there is ample time for
               lifting up the whole sweep of the personal life of
               faith.

The litanies mentioned above, indeed all the litanies in this collection, are
meant to be models or patterns which will inspire leaders of worship to use
this form of prayer imaginatively in the regular worship of their respective
congregations. The book is also, of course, a resource to be drawn upon by
those who take seriously the desire and hope expressed by the Second
Vatican Council: "that all the faithful should be led to that full, conscious,
and active participation in liturgical celebrations which is demanded by the
very nature of the liturgy."[27]

One further aspect of this book calls for comment. It will quickly become
obvious that no indication is given of the changes which have been made in
the various litanies. Since this is not an Oxford Book of Litanies, but an
ecumenical collection intended for widespread use in worship at the end of
the twentieth century, a great many alterations have proved necessary. These
changes and adaptations will, in each case, have been made for one or more
of the following reasons:

ecumenical applicability: in order to extend the contents and appeal of a
                              litany beyond the confines of a particular
                              denomination;

inclusive language: in order to avoid excessive use of such words as
                              "men" or "mankind" which no longer convey
                              the inclusive meaning they were certainly meant
                              to convey when used in the litany in its original
                              form;

contemporary references:	in order to broaden the categories mentioned in the various petitions of a litany and thereby to include more of life as we know it and live it in the closing years of this century;
intelligibility, brevity, and recitability:	in order to take into account the ways people pray in our day, the words they use, and the more concise forms of speech which are common to us;
inclusion of hymn stanzas:	in order to provide sung responses for use in liturgical settings where the traditional "sung litany" would not be familiar or acceptable;
division among several leaders:	in order to encourage greater diversity in the conduct and leadership of corporate prayer.

The classical form of the litany with its climax either in the Lord's Prayer or in a concluding collect said by the presiding minister has deliberately been avoided as an *invariable* model. This course has been followed for ecumenical and pastoral reasons, but those who wish to conclude a particular litany in either of these traditional ways may certainly do so.

A final word about leadership is in order. The person and presence of the leader are undoubtedly important. We have seen that the Puritans denounced the lifeless reading of collects from a book (in that instance the *Book of Common Prayer*) as "stinted prayer." The reading of litanies from *this* book can certainly fall prey to the same disease of lifelessness, and merit the same unpromising diagnosis! Careful preparation, sensitive adaptation, thoughtful integration with the other parts of the service, ample provision for silence or the free interpolation of additional petitions, unhurried pacing of the prayer, clear and audible reading, specificity without unnecessary divisiveness and generality without meaningless platitudes: these are all vital to the effective use of the litany as a form of corporate prayer. No leader is meant to preempt or stifle the priestly function of the people of God as they pray for the world. In like manner, no leader is meant to inhibit or cripple their prayer by poor and unthinking leadership.

This collection of litanies calls on God's mercy in all its height and depth and length and breadth. It also calls on those who pray in the service of the Church to take St. Teresa's words to heart, remembering also that Christ has no lips now but ours with which "to ask, for ourselves and on behalf of others, those things that are necessary for our life and our salvation."[28]

Christ has
No body now on earth but yours;
No hands but yours;
No feet but yours;
Yours are the eyes
Through which is to look out

Christ's compassion to the world;
Yours are the feet
With which he is to go about
Doing good;
Yours are the hands
With which he is to bless folk now.
              St. Teresa of Avila[29]

Notes

1. *Eucharist at Taizé (The Eucharistic Liturgy of Taizé)*, with an introductory essay by Max Thurian, Frère de Taizé; translated by John Arnold, Faith Press, London, 1962 (French original: 1959), p.2.
2. Ibid., p.1.
3. "A Prayer for all Conditions of Men" was first included in the *Book of Common Prayer* in 1662. It can now be found in the *Book of Common Prayer 1979* among the *Prayers and Thanksgivings* (pp. 814–5).
4. Romans 8:26 *(New English Bible)*. In place of "how we ought to pray," there is a variant reading which translates "what it is right to pray for."
5. Romans 12:1 (N.E.B.).
6. I Timothy 2:1–2 (N.E.B.).
7. *The First Apology*, para. 65. This early account of Christian worship in the city of Rome dates from about 155 A.D.
8. I Timothy 2:8 *(Revised Standard Version)*.
9. Faith and Order Paper No. 111, World Council of Churches, Geneva, 1982.
10. This quotation appears on the back cover of *Baptism, Eucharist and Ministry*.
11. Ibid., p. 14.
12. Ibid., p. 20.
13. Part of the *Baptismal Covenant* and of the *Renewal of Baptismal Vows* (Litany 128) in the *Book of Common Prayer 1979*, p. 305 and pp. 293–4, respectively.
14. *The Constitution on the Sacred Liturgy*, para. 53. This seminal document was promulgated by Pope Paul VI on December 4, 1963, after it had been adopted almost unanimously by the bishops assembled in Rome for the Second Vatican Council.
15. Chapter II, para. 45. The *Roman Missal* appeared in its definitive English translation in 1973.
16. Frederick William Faber (1814–1863) wrote this hymn in 1862. In his original version the first stanza began with the words, "Souls of men! why will ye scatter like a crowd of frightened sheep?"
17. The hymn appears in the *Lutheran Book of Worship* (no. 290) and in the *Hymnal 1940* (no. 304).
18. This sentence is a paraphrase of one of the prayers for mission in *Morning Prayer I* and *II* in the *Book of Common Prayer 1979* (pp. 58 and 101, respectively) Cf. I Timothy 2:4.
19. W.H. Auden wrote his *Hymn to St. Cecilia* in 1941. It was set to music by Benjamin Britten and the first public performance was given on November 22, 1942–appropriately enough Britten's birthday and St. Cecilia's Day!
20. Philippians 4:6 (R.S.V.).
21. Hebrews 7:25 (R.S.V.).
22. The *Book of Common Prayer 1979*, p. 148.
23. Luke 10:37 (R.S.V.).
24. In the *Lutheran Book of Worship* this text is set to the delightful Irish tune, *Slane*.
25. This may be sung to the early American tune *Distress* (to which it is set in the *Lutheran Book of Worship*) or to a more familiar tune in Long Meter.
26. Words of welcome to the newly baptized in the rite of *Holy Baptism* in the *Book of Common Prayer 1979*, p. 308.
27. *The Constitution on the Sacred Liturgy*, para. 14.

28. The Call to Worship in *Morning Prayer I* and *II* in the *Book of Common Prayer 1979*, pp. 41 and 79, respectively.
29. St. Teresa of Avila (1515–1582) is one of only two women among the great doctors (teachers) of the Catholic Church. She is celebrated as a mystic, as a writer on profound spiritual matters, and as a renewer of the Church. The 400th anniversary of her death was observed on October 4, 1982.

Prayer and Worship

Intercession: Ancient and Modern

• 1 The Great Litany**

*This may be said in its entirety, or Sections I and VI may be used together with a
selection of appropriate suffrages from Sections II, III, IV and V.*

I

O God the Father, Creator of heaven and earth:
Have mercy upon us.

O God the Son, Redeemer of the world:
Have mercy upon us.

O God the Holy Ghost, Sanctifier of the faithful:
Have mercy upon us.

O holy, blessed, and glorious Trinity, one God:
Have mercy upon us.

II

Remember not, Lord Christ, our offenses, nor the offenses of our forebears;
neither reward us according to our sins. Spare us, good Lord, spare thy
people, whom thou hast redeemed with thy most precious blood, and by thy
mercy preserve us for ever.
Spare us, good Lord.

From all evil and wickedness; from sin; from the crafts and assaults of the
devil; and from everlasting damnation:
Good Lord, deliver us.

**In all the litanies in this book, the responses in italics are to be said by the whole
congregation.*

From all blindness of heart; from pride, vainglory, and hypocrisy; from envy, hatred, and malice; and from all want of charity:
Good Lord, deliver us.

From all inordinate and sinful affections; and from all the deceits of the world, the flesh, and the devil:
Good Lord, deliver us.

From all false doctrine, heresy, and schism; from hardness of heart, and contempt of thy Word and commandment:
Good Lord, deliver us.

From lightning and tempest; from earthquake, fire, and flood; from plague, pestilence, and famine:
Good Lord, deliver us.

From all oppression, conspiracy, and rebellion; from violence, battle, and murder; and from dying suddenly and unprepared:
Good Lord, deliver us.

By the mystery of thy holy Incarnation; by thy holy Nativity and submission to the Law; by the Baptism, Fasting, and Temptation:
Good Lord, deliver us.

By thine Agony and Bloody Sweat; by thy Cross and Passion; by thy precious Death and Burial; by thy glorious Resurrection and Ascension; and by the Coming of the Holy Ghost:
Good Lord, deliver us.

In all time of our tribulation; in all time of our prosperity; in the hour of death, and in the day of judgment:
Good Lord, deliver us.

III

We sinners do beseech thee to hear us, O Lord God; and that it may please three to rule and govern thy holy Church Universal in the right way:
We beseech thee to hear us, good Lord.

That it may please thee to illumine all ministers of the Gospel, with true knowledge and understanding of thy Word; and that both by their preaching and living, they may set it forth, and show it accordingly:
We beseech thee to hear us, good Lord.

That it may please thee to bless and keep all the faithful:
We beseech thee to hear us, good Lord.

That it may please thee to send forth laborers into thy harvest, and to draw all of humanity into thy kingdom:

We beseech thee to hear us, good Lord.

That it may please thee to give to all people increase of grace to hear and receive thy Word, and to bring forth the fruits of the Spirit:
We beseech thee to hear us, good Lord.

That it may please thee to bring into the way of truth all such as have erred, and are deceived:
We beseech thee to hear us, good Lord.

That it may please thee to give us a heart to love and fear thee, and diligently to live after thy commandments:
We beseech thee to hear us, good Lord.

IV

That it may please thee so to rule the hearts of the servants, the President of the United States, and all others in authority, that they may do justice, and love mercy, and walk in the ways of truth:
We beseech thee to hear us, good Lord.

That it may please thee to make wars to cease in all the world; to give to all nations unity, peace, and concord; and to bestow freedom upon all peoples:
We beseech thee to hear us, good Lord.

That it may please thee to show thy pity upon all prisoners and captives, the homeless and the hungry, and all who are desolate and oppressed:
We beseech thee to hear us, good Lord.

That it may please thee to give and preserve to our use the bountiful fruits of the earth, so that in due time all may enjoy them:
We beseech thee to hear us, good Lord.

That it may please thee to inspire us, in our several callings, to do the work which thou givest us to do with singleness of heart as thy servants, and for the common good:
We beseech thee to hear us, good Lord.

That it may please thee to preserve all who are in danger by reason of their labor or their travel:
We beseech thee to hear us, good Lord.

That it may please thee to preserve, and provide for, all women in childbirth, young children and orphans, the widowed, and all whose homes are broken or torn by strife:
We beseech thee to hear us, good Lord.

That it may please thee to visit the lonely; to strengthen all who suffer in mind, body, and spirit; and to comfort with thy presence those who are failing and infirm:
We beseech thee to hear us, good Lord.

That it may please thee to support, help, and comfort all who are in danger, necessity, and tribulation:
We beseech thee to hear us, good Lord.

That it may please thee to have mercy upon people everywhere:
We beseech thee to hear us, good Lord.

V

That it may please thee to give us true repentance; to forgive us all our sins, negligences, and ignorances; and to endue us with the grace of thy Holy Spirit to amend our lives according to thy holy Word:
We beseech thee to hear us, good Lord.

That it may please thee to forgive our enemies, persecutors, and slanderers, and to turn their hearts:
We beseech thee to hear us, good Lord.

That it may please thee to strengthen such as do stand; to comfort and help the weak-hearted; to raise up those who fall; and finally to beat down Satan under our feet:
We beseech thee to hear us, good Lord.

That it may please thee to grant to all the faithful departed eternal life and peace:
We beseech thee to hear us, good Lord.

That it may please thee to grant that, in the fellowship of [_____ and] all the saints, we may attain to thy heavenly kingdom:
We beseech thee to hear us, good Lord.

VI

Son of God, we beseech thee to hear us.
Son of God, we beseech thee to hear us.

O Lamb of God, that takest away the sins of the world:
Have mercy upon us.

O Lamb of God, that takest away the sins of the world:
Have mercy upon us.

O Lamb of God, that takest away the sins of the world:
Grant us thy peace.

O Christ, hear us.
O Christ, hear us.

Lord, have mercy upon us.		Kyrie eleison.
Christ, have mercy upon us.	*or*	*Christe eleison.*
Lord, have mercy upon us.		Kyrie eleison.

The Officiant and People say together

Our Father, who art in heaven,
　　hallowed be thy Name,
　　thy kingdom come,
　　thy will be done,
　　　　on earth as it is in heaven.
Give us this day our daily bread.
And forgive us our trespasses,
　　as we forgive those who trespass against us.
And lead us not into temptation
　　but deliver us from evil. Amen.

O Lord, let thy mercy be showed upon us:
As we do put our trust in thee.

The Officiant concludes with the following or some other Collect.

Let us pray.

Almighty God, who hast promised to hear the petitions of those who ask in thy Son's Name: We beseech thee mercifully to incline thine ear to us who have now made our prayers and supplications unto thee; and grant that those things which we have asked faithfully according to thy will, may be obtained effectually, to the relief of our necessity, and to the setting forth of thy glory; through Jesus Christ our Lord. *Amen.*

The Officiant may add other Prayers, and end the Litany, saying

The grace of our Lord Jesus Christ, and the love of God, and the fellowship of the Holy Ghost, be with us all evermore. *Amen.*

THE BOOK OF COMMON PRAYER 1979*
*An asterisk at the end of a litany indicates that further information is to be found in the *Notes* at the end of the book.

• 2 A Bidding Prayer

After each period of silent prayer, the Leader may also add the words, "Lord, in your mercy," *and the People respond,* "hear our prayer."

Good Christian People, I bid your prayers for Christ's holy catholic Church, the blessed company of all faithful people: that it may please God to confirm and strengthen it in purity of faith, in holiness of life, and in perfectness of love, and to restore to it the witness of visible unity.

Silence

I bid your prayers more especially for that branch of the same planted by God in this land, whereof we are members; that in all things it may work according to God's will, serve him faithfully, and worship him acceptably.

Silence

I bid your prayers for the President of these United States, and for the Governor of this State, and for all that are in authority; that all, and every one of them, may serve truly in their several callings to the glory of God, and the edifying and well-governing of the people, remembering the account they shall be called upon to give at the last great day.

Silence

I bid your prayers for all ministers of God's Holy Word and Sacraments; that they may minister faithfully and shine as lights in the world, in all things adorning the doctrine of God our Savior.

Silence

I bid your prayers for a due supply of persons fitted to serve God in the Ministry and in the State; and to that end, as well as for the good education of all the youth of this land, you shall pray for all schools, colleges, and seminaries of sound and godly learning, and for all whose hands are open for their maintenance; that whatsoever tends to the advancement of true religion and useful learning may for ever flourish and abound.

Silence

I bid your prayers for all the people of these United States, that they may live in the true faith and fear of God, and abound in charity one towards another.

Silence

I bid your prayers for all who travel by land, sea, or air; for all prisoners and captives; for all who are in sickness or in sorrow; for all who have fallen into grievous sin; for all who, through temptation, ignorance, helplessness, grief, trouble, dread, or the near approach of death, especially need our prayers.

Silence

I bid your prayers for this congregation, that we may have grace to direct our lives after the good example of God's saints; that, this life ended, we may be made partakers with them of the glorious resurrection, and the life everlasting.

Silence

And now, beloved in Christ, summing up all our petitions in the words which he himself taught us, we are bold to say,

Our Father, who art in heaven,
  hallowed be thy Name,
  thy kingdom come,
  thy will be done,
    on earth as it is in heaven.
Give us this day our daily bread.
And forgive us our trespasses,
  as we forgive those who trespass against us.
And lead us not into temptation,
  but deliver us from evil.
For thine is the kingdom,
  and the power, and the glory,
  for ever and ever. Amen.

THE BOOK OF COMMON PRAYER 1928*

•3 Prayer of the Church

Almighty God, giver of all things, with gladness we give thanks for all your goodness. We bless you for the love which has created and which sustains us from day to day. We praise you for the gift of your Son our Savior, through whom you have made known your will and grace. We thank you for the Holy Spirit, the comforter; for your holy Church; for the means of grace; for the lives of all faithful and good people; and for the hope of the life to come. Help us to treasure in our hearts all that our Lord has done for us, and enable us to show our thankfulness by lives that are wholly given to your service.
Hear us, good Lord.

Save and defend your whole Church, purchased with the precious blood of Christ. Give it pastors and ministers filled with your Spirit, and strengthen it through the Word and the holy sacraments. Make it perfect in love and in all good works, and establish it in the faith delivered to the saints. Sanctify and

unite your people in all the world, that one holy Church may bear witness to you, the creator and redeemer of all.
Hear us, good Lord.

Give your wisdom and heavenly grace to all pastors and to those who hold office in your Church, that, by their faithful service, faith may abound and your kingdom increase.
Hear us, good Lord.

Send the light of your truth into all the earth. Raise up faithful servants of Christ to labor in the Gospel both at home and in distant lands.
Hear us, good Lord.

In your mercy strengthen the younger churches and support them in times of trial. Make them steadfast, abounding in the work of the Lord, and let their faith and zeal for the Gospel refresh and renew the witness of your people everywhere.
Hear us, good Lord.

Preserve our nation in justice and honor, that we may lead a peaceable life of integrity. Grant health and favor to all who bear office in our land, especially to the President of the United States, the Governor of this State, and all those who make, administer, and judge our laws, and help them to serve this people according to your holy will.
Hear us, good Lord.

Take from us all hatred and prejudice, give us the spirit of love, and dispose our days in your peace. Prosper the labors of those who take counsel for the nations of the world, that mutual understanding and common endeavor may be increased among all peoples.
Hear us, good Lord.

Bless the schools of the Church and all colleges, universities, and centers of research and those who teach in them. Bestow your wisdom in such measure that people may serve you in Church and state and that our common life may be conformed to the rule of your truth and justice.
Hear us, good Lord.

Sanctify our homes with your presence and joy. Keep our children in the covenant of their baptism and enable their parents to rear them in a life of faith and devotion. By the spirit of affection and service unite the members of all families, that they may show your praise in our land and in all the world.
Hear us, good Lord.

Let your blessing rest upon the seedtime and harvest, the commerce and industry, the leisure and rest, the arts and culture of our people. Take under your special protection those whose work is difficult or dangerous, and be

with all who lay their hands to any useful task. Give them just rewards for their labor and the knowledge that their work is good in your sight.
Hear us, good Lord.

Special supplications, intercessions, and thanksgivings may be made here.

Comfort with the grace of your Holy Spirit all who are in sorrow or need, sickness or adversity. Remember those who suffer persecution for the faith. Have mercy on those to whom death draws near. Bring consolation to those in sorrow or mourning. And to all grant a measure of your love, taking them into your tender care.
Hear us, good Lord.

We remember with thanksgiving those who have loved and served you in your Church on earth, who now rest from their labors [especially those most dear to us, whom we name before you now _____]. Keep us in fellowship with all your saints, and bring us at last to the joy of your heavenly kingdom.
Hear us, good Lord.

All these things and whatever else you see that we need, grant us, Father, for the sake of him who died and rose again, and now lives and reigns with you in the unity of the Holy Spirit, one God forever. *Amen.*

THE LUTHERAN BOOK OF WORSHIP

•4 Litany of Intercession

The Litany of Intercession may be said in its entirety or selectively. The response, "Hear our prayer, O Lord," may be used after each petition instead of the variety of responses provided.

O Lord our God: you hear our prayers before we speak, and answer before we know our need. Though we cannot pray, may your Spirit pray in us, drawing us to you and toward our neighbors on earth. *Amen.*

We pray for the whole creation: may all things work together for good, until, by your design, your children inherit the earth and order it wisely.
Let the whole creation praise you, Lord and God.

We pray for the Church of Jesus Christ; that, begun, maintained, and promoted by your Spirit, it may be true, engaging, glad, and active, doing your will.
Let the Church be always faithful, Lord and God.

We pray for men and women who serve the Church in special ways, preaching, ruling, showing charity; that they may never lose heart, but have all hope encouraged.
Let leadership be strong, Lord and God.

We pray for people who do not believe, who are shaken by doubt, or have turned against you. Open their eyes to see beyond our broken fellowship the wonders of your love displayed in Jesus of Nazareth; and to follow when he calls them.
Conquer doubt with faith, O God.

We pray for peace in the world. Disarm weapons, silence guns, and put out ancient hate that smolders still, or flames in sudden conflict. Create goodwill among every race and nation.
Bring peace to earth, O God.

We pray for all who must go to war, and for those who will not go: may they have conviction, and charity toward one another.
Guard the brave everywhere, O God.

We pray for enemies, as Christ commanded; for those who oppose us or scheme against us, who are also children of your love. May we be kept from infectious hate or sick desire for vengeance.
Make friends of enemies, O God.

We pray for those involved in world government, in agencies of control or compassion, who work for the reconciling of nations: keep them hopeful, and work with them for peace.
Unite our broken world, O God.

We pray for those who govern us, who make, administer, or judge our laws. May this country ever be a land of free and able leaders who welcome exiles and work for justice.
Govern those who govern us, O God.

We pray for poor people who are hungry, or are housed in cramped places. Increase in us, and all who prosper, concern for the disinherited.
Care for the poor, O God.

We pray for social outcasts; for those excluded by their own militance or by the harshness of others. Give us grace to accept those our world names unacceptable, and so show your mighty love.
Welcome the alienated, O God.

We pray for sick people who suffer pain, or struggle with demons of the mind, who silently cry out for healing: may they be patient, brave, and trusting.
Heal the sick and troubled, O God.

We pray for the dying, who face the final mystery: may they enjoy light and life intensely, keep dignity, and greet death unafraid, believing in your love. *Have mercy on the dying, O God.*

We pray for those whose tears are not yet dry, who listen for familiar voices and look for still familiar faces: in loss, may they affirm all that you promise in Jesus, who prepares a place for us within your spacious love. *Comfort those who sorrow, O God.*

We pray for people who are alone and lonely, who have no one to call in easy friendship: may they be remembered, befriended, and know your care for them. *Visit lonely people, O God.*

We pray for families, for parents and children: may they enjoy each other, honor freedoms, and forgive as happily as we are all forgiven in your huge mercy. *Keep families in your love, O God.*

We pray for young and old: give impatient youth true vision, and experienced age openness to new things. Let both praise your name. *Join youth and age together, O God.*

We pray for people everywhere: may they come into their own as children of God, and inherit the kingdom prepared in Jesus Christ, the Lord of all, and Savior of the world. *Hear our prayers, almighty God, in the name of Jesus Christ, who prays with us and for us, to whom be praise forever. Amen.*

THE WORSHIPBOOK

•5 The Whole State of Christ's Church

Almighty God, who hast taught us to make prayers, supplications, and intercessions for all; hear us when we pray:

That it may please thee to inspire continually the universal Church with the spirit of truth, unity, and concord: *Hear us, we beseech thee.*

That it may please thee to grant that all they that do confess thy holy name may agree in the truth of thy holy Word, and live in unity and godly love: *Hear us, we beseech thee.*

That it may please thee to lead all nations in the paths of righteousness and peace:

Hear us, we beseech thee.

That it may please thee to direct all those in authority, especially _____, our _____, that under them the world may be godly and quietly governed:
Hear us, we beseech thee.

That it may please thee to give grace to all ministers and leaders of the Church, especially to thy servant _____, our _____, that by their life and doctrine they may set forth thy true and living Word, and rightly and duly administer thy Holy Sacraments:
Hear us, we beseech thee.

That it may please thee to guide and prosper all those who are laboring for the spread of thy Gospel among the nations, and to enlighten with thy Spirit all places of education and learning:
Hear us, we beseech thee.

That it may please thee that through thy heavenly benediction we may be saved from drought, scarcity and famine, and may with thankful hearts enjoy the fruits of the earth in their season:
Hear us, we beseech thee.

That it may please thee to give all thy people thy heavenly grace; and specially to this congregation here present; that, with meek heart and due reverence, they may hear, and receive thy holy Word; truly serving thee in holiness and righteousness all the days of their life:
Hear us, we beseech thee.

That it may please thee of thy goodness, O Lord, to comfort and succor all those who in this transitory life are in trouble, sorrow, need, sickness, or any other adversity:
Hear us, we beseech thee.

That it may please thee to grant to all thy servants departed this life in thy faith and fear, mercy, everlasting light, and peace:
Hear us, we beseech thee.

That it may please thee to give us grace that we may be partakers of thy heavenly kingdom with all thy saints, patriarchs, prophets, apostles, and martyrs:
Hear us, we beseech thee.

Almighty God, the fountain of all wisdom, who knowest our necessities before we ask, and our ignorance in asking: We beseech thee to have compassion upon our infirmities; and those things, which for our unworthiness we dare not, and for our blindness we cannot ask, vouchsafe to give us, for the worthiness of thy Son Jesus Christ our Lord. *Amen.*

THE CEYLON LITURGY*

•6 The Church and the World

Let us pray for the Church and for the world.

Grant, Almighty God, that all who confess your Name may be united in your truth, live together in your love, and reveal your glory in the world.

Silence

Lord, in your mercy:
Hear our prayer.

Guide the people of this land, and of all the nations, in the ways of justice and peace; that we may honor one another and serve the common good.

Silence

Lord, in your mercy:
Hear our prayer.

Give us all a reverence for the earth as your own creation, that we may use its resources rightly in the service of others and to your honor and glory.

Silence

Lord, in your mercy:
Hear our prayer.

Bless all whose lives are closely linked with ours, and grant that we may serve Christ in them, and love one another as he loves us.

Silence

Lord, in your mercy:
Hear our prayer.

Comfort and heal all those who suffer in body, mind, or spirit; give them courage and hope in their troubles, and bring them the joy of your salvation.

Silence

Lord, in your mercy:
Hear our prayer.

We commend to your mercy all who have died, that your will for them may be fulfilled; and we pray that we may share with all your saints in your eternal kingdom.

Silence

Merciful Father, accept these prayers, for the sake of your Son, our Savior Jesus Christ. Amen.

THE BOOK OF COMMON PRAYER 1979

•7 A General Litany

In peace, we pray to you, Lord God.

Silence

For all people in their daily life and work:
For our families, friends, and neighbors, and for those who are alone.

For this community, the nation, and the world:
For all who work for justice, freedom, and peace.

For the just and proper use of your creation:
For the victims of hunger, fear, injustice, and oppression.

For all who are in danger, sorrow, or any kind of trouble:
For those who minister to the sick, the friendless, and the needy.

For the peace and unity of the Church of God:
For all who proclaim the Gospel, and all who seek the Truth.

For [*N.* our Presiding Bishop, and *N. (N.)* our Bishop(s); and for] all bishops and other ministers:
For all who serve God in his Church.

For the special needs and concerns of this congregation.

Silence

The People may add their own petitions.

Hear us Lord:
For your mercy is great.

We thank you, Lord, for all the blessings of this life.

Silence

The People may add their own thanksgivings.

We will exalt you, O God our King:
And praise your Name for ever and ever.

We pray for all who have died, thay they may have a place in your eternal kingdom.

Silence

The People may add their own petitions.

Lord, let your loving – kindness be upon them;
Who put their trust in you.

We pray to you also for the forgiveness of our sins.

Silence may be kept.

Have mercy upon us, most merciful Father;
in your compassion forgive us our sins,
known and unknown,
things done and left undone;
and so uphold us by your Spirit
that we may live and serve you in newness of life,
to the honor and glory of your Name;
through Jesus Christ our Lord.
Amen.

The Minister concludes with an absolution or with an assurance of pardon.

THE BOOK OF COMMON PRAYER 1979

•8 The Prayers of God's People– South Africa

Particular intentions may be mentioned before this prayer but it is said without interpolation.

Father, we are your children, your Spirit lives in us and we are in your Spirit: hear us, for it is your Spirit who speaks through us as we pray.
Lord, hear us.

Father, you created the heavens and the earth: bless the produce of our land and the works of our hands.
Lord, hear us.

Father, you created the human family in your own image: teach us to honor you in our brothers and sisters.
Lord, hear us.

Father, you provide for all your children: grant good rains for our crops.
Lord, hear us.

Father, you inspired the prophets of old: grant that your Church may faithfully proclaim your truth to the world.
Lord, hear us.

Father, you sent your Son into the world: reveal him to others through his life in us.
Lord, hear us.

Lord Jesus, you called the apostles to be fishers of men: bless the bishops of this Province, especially _____ our bishop and all other ministers of your Church.

Christ, hear us.

Lord Jesus, for your sake men and women forsook all and followed you: call many to serve you in Religious Communities and in the ordained ministry of your Church.
Christ, hear us.

Lord Jesus, you called men and women to be your disciples: deepen in each of us a sense of vocation.
Christ, hear us.

You prayed that your Church may be one: unite all Christians so that the world may believe you have sent us.
Christ, hear us.

You forgave the thief on the cross: bring to all penitence and reconciliation.
Christ, hear us.

You gave us your peace: bring the people of this world to live in true community and concord.
Christ, hear us.

You taught us through Paul, your apostle, to pray for all kings and rulers: bless and guide all who are in authority.
Christ, hear us.

You were rich yet for our sake became poor: move those who have wealth to share generously with those who are poor.
Christ, hear us.

You sat among the learned, listening and asking them questions: inspire all who teach and all who learn.
Christ, hear us.

You cured by your healing touch and word: heal the sick and bless all who minister to them.
Christ, hear us.

You were unjustly condemned by Pontius Pilate: strengthen our brothers and sisters who are suffering injustice and persecution.
Christ, hear us.

You lived as an exile in Egypt: be with all migrant workers and protect their families.
Christ, hear us.

You open and none can shut: open the gates of your kingdom to those who have died without hearing your Gospel.
Christ, hear us.

You have been glorified in the lives of innumerable saints: give us strength through their prayers to follow in their footsteps.
Christ, hear us.

Father, we know that you are good and that you hear all those who call upon you: give to us and to all what is best so that we may glorify you through your Son, Jesus Christ our Lord, who is alive and reigns with you and the Holy Spirit, one God, now and for ever. *Amen.*

THE ANGLICAN CHURCH OF THE PROVINCE OF SOUTH AFRICA*

•9 The Prayers of God's People – Iran

Let us pray for the universal Church of Christ and for all people according to their needs.

Silence

O God, grant us your peace:
And salvation to all the world.

Strengthen your Church:
And increase it day by day.

Guide all Christians in the way of unity:
And grant that we may grow in your love.

Give your grace to all ministers of your Church, especially your servant
_____, our _____:
And strengthen them in the ministry of your Word and Sacraments.

Bless, we pray, all those who work for the spread of your Gospel in the world:
And encourage the messengers of your saving love.

Direct the minds of those who are seeking Christ:
And make them strong in faith.

Guide the world in the way of peace:
And direct the leaders of the nations.

Bring all peoples into the path of justice and harmony:
And into obedience to your commands.

Direct all those in authority, especially the President of the United States:
And give them the spirit of service.

May this city and state flourish:
For the welfare and blessing of the people.

Look with favor upon universities and schools:
That knowledge may be acquired for your glory and the benefit of humanity.

Heal the sick and the afflicted:
And help all those in trouble.

May those who are near death have the assurance of your presence:
That they may entrust themselves to your loving care.

Give your strength to those who dedicate themselves to the healing of the sick:
And help them to minister to all who suffer pain.

May the wants of the needy be supplied, and the hungry be fed:
And help us to relieve their suffering.

Grant us your grace that we may hear your Holy Word:
And help us both to receive and fulfill it.

We thank you for your servants who have died in faith:
And pray that we may follow their good examples, and share with them in your eternal kingdom. Amen.

THE ANGLICAN CHURCH IN IRAN*

• 10 The Prayers of God's People – The United States

Father, we pray for your holy Catholic Church:
That we all may be one.

Grant that every member of the Church may truly and humbly serve you:
That your Name may be glorified by all people.

We pray for all bishops, priests, and deacons:
That they may be faithful ministers of your Word and Sacraments.

We pray for all who govern and hold authority in the nations of the world:
That there may be justice and peace on the earth.

Give us grace to do your will in all that we undertake:
That our works may find favor in your sight.

Have compassion on those who suffer from any grief or trouble:
That they may be delivered from their distress.

Give to the departed eternal rest:
Let light perpetual shine upon them.

We praise you for your saints who have entered into joy:
May we also come to share in your heavenly kingdom.

Let us pray for our own needs and those of others.

Silence

The People may add their own petitions.

The Leader concludes with one of the following Collects.

Almighty and eternal God, ruler of all things in heaven and earth: Mercifully accept the prayers of your people, and strengthen us to do your will; through Jesus Christ our Lord. *Amen.*

Heavenly Father, you have promised to hear what we ask in the Name of your Son: Accept and fulfill our petitions, we pray, not as we ask in our ignorance, nor as we deserve in our sinfulness, but as you know and love us in your Son Jesus Christ our Lord. *Amen.*

Almighty God, you have given us grace at this time with one accord to make our common supplication to you; and you have promised that when two or three are gathered together in your Name you will grant their requests. Fulfill now, O Lord, the desires and petitions of your servants, as may be most expedient for them, granting us in this world knowledge of your truth, and in the world to come, life everlasting. *Amen.*

Hasten, O Father, the coming of your kingdom; and grant that we your servants, who now live by faith, may with joy behold your Son at his coming in glorious majesty; even Jesus Christ, our only Mediator and Advocate. *Amen.*

THE BOOK OF COMMON PRAYER 1979

•11 The Prayers of God's People – France

We pray, Lord, for this country and all who live here, the poor, the immigrants, old people and children, the victims of society and of evil in our midst: save and defend them all.
Lord, in your mercy, hear our prayer.

We pray for the peoples who are victims of our national policies, and of the inequalities in the world: establish justice by your power so that all the nations may enjoy the good things you have given us.
Lord, in your mercy, hear our prayer.

We pray for the hungry and starving, victims of constant malnutrition: move us by your self-giving love to share with those in need.
Lord, in your mercy, hear our prayer.

We pray for those who hate and persecute our Christian brothers and sisters on account of their faith and their service of the poorest: turn their hearts to good, and give courage and endurance to their victims.
Lord, in your mercy, hear our prayer.

We pray for those newly converted and for those discovering your love: strengthen them in faith and hope, deliver them in temptation, and forgive them all their sin.

Lord, in your mercy, hear our prayer.

We pray for those far away, but dear to us: gather us again, and bring us to your Kingdom, for you are the Lord of all that live.
Lord, in your mercy, hear our prayer.

PRAISE GOD: COMMON PRAYER AT TAIZÉ*

• 12 The Eighteen Benedictions

Eternal God, open my lips:
That my mouth may declare your praise.

We praise you, Lord our God and God of all generations: God of Abraham, God of Isaac, God of Jacob; great, mighty, and awesome God, God supreme.

Master of all the living, your ways are ways of love. You remember the faithfulness of our ancestors, and in love bring redemption to their children's children for the sake of your name.

You are our King and our Help, our Savior and our Shield.
Blessed is the Lord, the Shield of Abraham.

Eternal is your might, O Lord; all life is your gift; great is your power to save!

With love you sustain the living, with great compassion give life to all. You send help to the falling and healing to the sick; you bring freedom to the captive and keep faith with those who sleep in the dust.

Who is like you, Lord of might? Who is your equal, O King of life and death, Source of salvation?
Blessed is the Lord, the Source of life.

We sanctify your name on earth, even as all things, to the ends of time and space, proclaim your holiness; and in the words of the prophet we say:
Holy, Holy, Holy is the Lord of Hosts; the fullness of the whole earth is his glory!

They respond to your glory with blessing:
Blessed is the glory of God in heaven and earth.

And this is your sacred word:
The Lord shall reign for ever; your God, O Zion, from generation to generation. Hallelujah!

To all generations we will make known your greatness, and to all eternity proclaim your holiness. Your praise, O God, shall never depart from our lips.
Blessed is the Lord, the holy God.

You favor us with knowledge and teach mortals understanding. May you continue to favor us with knowledge, understanding, and insight.
Blessed is the Lord, gracious Giver of knowledge.

Help us to return, our Maker, to your Law; draw us near, O Soverign God, to your service; and bring us back into your presence in perfect repentance.
Blessed is the Lord, who calls for repentance.

Forgive us, our Creator, when we have sinned; pardon us, our King, when we transgress; for you are a forgiving God.
Blessed is the Lord, the gracious God, whose forgiveness is abundant.

Look upon our affliction and help us in our need; O mighty Redeemer, redeem us speedily for your name's sake.
Blessed is the Lord, the Redeemer of Israel.

Heal us, O Lord, and we shall be healed; save us, and we shall be saved; grant us a perfect healing from all our wounds.
Blessed is the Lord, the Healer of the sick.

Bless this year, O Lord our God, and let its produce bring us well-being. Bestow your blessing on the earth and satisfy us with your goodness.
Blessed is the Lord, from whom all blessings flow.

Sound the great horn to proclaim freedom, inspire us to strive for the liberation of the oppressed, and let the song of liberty be heard in the four corners of the earth.
Blessed is the Lord, Redeemer of the oppressed.

Pour your spirit upon the rulers of all lands; guide them, that they may govern justly. O may you alone reign over us in steadfast love and compassion!
Blessed is the Lord, the King, who loves righteousness and justice.

Have mercy, O Lord our God, upon the righteous and faithful of all peoples, and upon all of us. Uphold all who faithfully put their trust in you, and grant that we may always be numbered among them.
Blessed is the Lord, the Staff and Support of the righteous.

And turn in compassion to Jerusalem, your city. Let there be peace in her gates, quietness in the hearts of her inhabitants. Let your Law go forth from Zion and your word from Jerusalem.
Blessed is the Lord, who gives peace to Jerusalem.

Cause the plant of justice to spring up soon. Let the light of deliverance shine forth according to your word, for we await your deliverance all the day.
Blessed is the Lord, who will cause the light of deliverance to dawn for all the world.

Hear our voice, O Lord our God; have compassion upon us, and accept our prayer with favor and mercy, for you are a God who hears prayer and supplication.
Blessed is the Lord, who hearkens to prayer.

Be gracious, O Lord our God, to your people, and receive our prayers with love. May our worship always be acceptable to you.

Fill us with the knowledge that you are near to all who seek you in truth. Let our eyes behold your presence in Zion and in the midst of your people. *Blessed is the Lord, whose presence gives life to all Zion's people.*

We gratefully acknowledge that you are the Lord our God and God of all generations. You are the Rock of our life, the Power that shields us in every age. We thank you and sing your praises: for our lives, which are in your hand; for our souls, which are in your keeping; for the signs of your presence we encounter every day; and for your wondrous gifts at all times, morning, noon, and night. You are Goodness: your mercies never end; you are Compassion: your love will never fail. You have always been our hope. *For all these things, O Sovereign God, let your name be for ever exalted and blessed.*

Peace, happiness, and blessing; grace and love and mercy: may these descend on us, on Zion and on all the world.

Bless us, our Creator, one and all, with the light of your presence; for by that light, O God, you have revealed to us the law of life: to love kindness and justice and mercy, to seek blessing, life, and peace.

O bless your people with enduring peace!
Praised be the Lord, who blesses his people with peace. Amen.

GATES OF PRAYER: THE NEW UNION PRAYER BOOK*

•13 The Litany of Pope Gelasius

Hear us, Lord, and have mercy.
With every confidence we call on the Father of the Only-Begotten, the Son
    of the eternal Father, and our Lord the Holy Spirit.
Kyrie eleison. (Lord, have mercy.)

For the spotless Church of the living God, everywhere throughout the world,
    we appeal to the God who is rich in goodness.
Kyrie eleison.

For God's holy priests, the ministers at the sacred altar, and all the peoples
    that worship the true God, we offer our prayers to Christ the Lord.
Kyrie eleison.

For those who preach the true word as they ought, we pray with special
    earnestness to God's Word in his infinite wisdom.
Kyrie eleison.

For all who, keeping themselves chaste in soul and body to obtain the
  kingdom of heaven, spend themselves in God's service, we implore the
  Giver of spiritual gifts.
Kyrie eleison.

For Christians in public office who labor for justice and equity, we beseech
  the omnipotent God.
Kyrie eleison.

For mild and pleasant weather, for rain at the time it is needed, for healthy
  and gentle winds and for the seasons to follow one another to our
  advantage, we entreat the Ruler of the universe.
Kyrie eleison.

To those who have acquired some knowledge of Christianity and some desire
  for its heavenly grace, we beg the all-powerful God to show his mercy.
Kyrie eleison.

For those beset by the frailty inherent in this weak human nature, we ask our
  Redeemer's mercy.
Kyrie eleison.

For those who are forced to live abroad, those persecuted by rulers who
  wield their power unjustly, and those harassed by enemy action, we
  implore our Lord and Savior.
Kyrie eleison.

For those deceived by false teaching and crooked reasoning and for those
  sunk in superstition, we make our prayer to the God of truth.
Kyrie eleison.

To those whose faith moves them to relieve the wants of the needy, we pray
  the Lord to show his great mercy.
Kyrie eleison.

For all who ever cross the threshold of this holy house, and for those
  assembled here now in humble devotion, we offer our prayers to the Lord
  in his glory.
Kyrie eleison.

For the cleansing of our bodies and souls and the forgiveness of all our sins,
  we entreat the God of boundless compassion.
Kyrie eleison.

For rest for the souls of all the faithful, especially those ministers of the
  Lord who have served this church, we pray the Lord of the spirits and
  Judge of all flesh.
Kyrie eleison.

Bodies dead to sin and souls alive by faith:
  Grant us, Lord, grant us.

Holy fear and true love:
Grant us, Lord, grant us.

Lives that please you, deaths you can approve of:
Grant us, Lord, grant us.

Angels to bring us peace and saints to assist us:
Grant us, Lord, grant us.

Our lives and all that we have we owe to the Lord. He gave them, he
increased them, he gives us the means to sustain them. To his mercy we
commend them, and to the judgment of his providence.
Lord, have mercy. Amen.

ROME, LATE 5th CENTURY*

•14 Prayer for All Needs

We beg you, Lord,
to help and defend us.

Deliver the oppressed. *Amen.*
Pity the insignificant. *Amen.*
Raise the fallen. *Amen.*
Show yourself to the needy. *Amen.*
Heal the sick. *Amen.*
Bring back those of your people who have gone astray. *Amen.*
Feed the hungry. *Amen.*
Lift up the weak. *Amen.*
Take off the prisoners' chains. *Amen.*

May every nation come to know
that you alone are God,
that Jesus Christ is your Child,
that we are your people, the sheep that you pasture. *Amen.*

CLEMENT OF ROME, LATE 1st CENTURY*

•15 Litany of Peace

In peace, let us pray to the Lord.
Lord, have mercy.

For the peace from above, and for our salvation, let us pray to the Lord.
Lord, have mercy.

For the peace of the whole world, for the well-being of the Church of God, and for the unity of all, let us pray to the Lord.
Lord, have mercy.

For this holy house, and for all who offer here their worship and praise, let us pray to the Lord.
Lord, have mercy.

For _____, for our pastor(s) in Christ, for all servants of the Church, and for all the people, let us pray to the Lord.
Lord, have mercy.

For our public servants, for the government and those who protect us, that they may be upheld and strengthened in every good deed, let us pray to the Lord.
Lord, have mercy.

For those who work to bring peace, justice, health, and protection in this and every place, let us pray to the Lord.
Lord, have mercy.

For those who bring offerings, those who do good works in this congregation, those who toil, those who sing, and all the people here present who await from the Lord great and abundant mercy, let us pray to the Lord.
Lord, have mercy.

For favorable weather, for an abundance of the fruits of the earth, and for peaceful times, let us pray to the Lord.
Lord, have mercy.

For our deliverance from all affliction, wrath, danger, and need, let us pray to the Lord.
Lord, have mercy.

For the faithful who have gone before us and are at rest, let us give thanks to the Lord.
Alleluia.

Help, save, comfort, and defend us, gracious Lord.

Silence for meditation

Rejoicing in the fellowship of all the saints, let us commend ourselves, one another, and our whole life to Christ, our Lord.
To you, O Lord.

O God, from whom come all holy desires, all good counsels, and all just works: Give to us, your servants, that peace which the world cannot give, that our hearts may be set to obey your commandments; and also that we, being defended from the fear of our enemies, may live in peace and quietness; through the merits of Jesus Christ our Savior, who lives and reigns with you and the Holy Spirit, God forever. *Amen.*

THE LUTHERAN BOOK OF WORSHIP*

•16 The Lutheran Litany

Lord, have mercy.
Lord, have mercy.

Christ, have mercy.
Christ, have mercy.

Lord, have mercy.
Lord, have mercy.

O Christ, hear us.
In mercy hear us.

God, the Father in heaven:
Have mercy on us.

God, the Son, redeemer of the world:
Have mercy on us.

God, the Holy Spirit:
Have mercy on us.

Holy Trinity, one God:
Have mercy on us.

Be gracious to us.
Spare us, good Lord.

Be gracious to us.
Spare us, good Lord.

From all sin, from all error, from all evil;
from the cunning assaults of the devil;
from an unprepared and evil death;
Good Lord, deliver us.

From war, bloodshed, and violence;
from corrupt and unjust government;
from sedition and treason:
Good Lord, deliver us.

From epidemic, drought, and famine;
from fire and flood, earthquake, lightning and storm;
and from everlasting death:
Good Lord, deliver us.

By the mystery of your incarnation;
by your holy birth:
Help us, good Lord.

By your baptism, fasting, and temptation;
by your agony and bloody sweat;
by your cross and suffering;
by your death and burial:
Help us, good Lord.

By your resurrection and ascension;
by the gift of the Holy Spirit:
Help us, good Lord.

In all time of our tribulation;
in all time of our prosperity;
in the hour of death;
and in the day of judgment:
Save us, good Lord.

Though unworthy, we implore you:
To hear us, Lord our God.

To rule and govern your holy catholic Church;
to guide all servants of your Church in the love of your Word and in holiness
of life;
to put an end to all schisms and causes of offense to those who would
believe;
and to bring into the way of truth all who have gone astray:
We implore you to hear us, good Lord.

To beat down Satan under our feet;
to send faithful workers into your harvest;
to accompany your Word with your Spirit and power;
to raise up those who fall and to strengthen those who stand;
and to comfort and help the fainthearted and the distressed:
We implore you to hear us, good Lord.

To give all nations justice and peace;
to preserve our country from discord and strife;
to direct and guard those who have civil authority;
and to bless and guide all our people:
We implore you to hear us, good Lord.

To behold and help all who are in danger, need, or tribulation;
to protect and guide all who travel;
to preserve and provide for all women in childbirth;

to watch over children and to guide the young;
to heal the sick and to strengthen their families and friends;
to bring reconciliation to families in discord;
to provide for the unemployed and for all in need;
to be merciful to all who are imprisoned;
to support, comfort, and guide all orphans, widowers, and widows;
and to have mercy on all your peopple:
We implore you to hear us, good Lord.

To forgive our enemies, persecutors, and slanderers, and to reconcile us to
    them;
to help us use wisely the fruits and treasures of the earth, the sea, and the
    air;
and graciously to hear our prayers:
We implore you to hear us, good Lord.

Lord Jesus Christ, Son of God:
We implore you to hear us.

Lamb of God, you take away the sin of the world:
Have mercy on us.

Lamb of God, you take away the sin of the world:
Have mercy on us.

Lamb of God, you take away the sin of the world:
Give us peace. Amen.

O Christ, hear us.
In mercy hear us.

Lord, have mercy.
Lord, have mercy.

Christ, have mercy.
Christ, have mercy.

Lord, have mercy.
Lord, have mercy.

THE LUTHERAN BOOK OF WORSHIP*

•17 From the *Preces Privatae*

O Thou that art the hope of all the ends of the earth:
Remember all thy creation for good, and visit the world with thy compassion.

O Thou preserver of men, O Lord thou lover of man:
Remember all our race, and have mercy on all.

O helper of the helpless, refuge in due time of trouble:

Remember all that are in necessity, and need thy help.

O Thou wholesome defense of thine anointed:
Remember thy congregations which Thou hast purchased and established of old.

O King of the nations unto the ends of the earth:
Strengthen all the commonwealths of the world, and make wars to cease in all the earth.

O Lord, on whom the isles do wait and on whom they hope:
Deliver this nation from all tribulation, peril and necessity.

O Lord of lords, Prince of princes:
Remember all to whom Thou hast given rule and authority on the earth.

O God not of us only but also of our seed:
Remember our children among us that they may increase in wisdom and in favor both with Thee and with men.

O Thou that willest we provide for our own:
Remember, Lord, our kindred according to the flesh and do them good.

O Thou that hast written that they that are careless of their own house are worse than infidels:
Remember according to thy favor all in our households.

O Thou that willest we overcome evil with good and pray for them which despitefully use us:
Have mercy on our enemies, Lord, as on ourselves and bring them to thy heavenly kingdom.

O Thou which grantest the prayers of thy servants one for another:
Remember, O Lord, for good all that bear us in mind in their prayers, and all we have promised to bear in mind in our prayers.

And may the Lord bless us and keep us:
The Lord make his face to shine upon us
    and be gracious unto us:
The Lord lift up his countenance upon us
    and give us peace. Amen.

LANCELOT ANDREWES, EARLY 17th CENTURY*

• 18 Litany on the Lord's Prayer

Our Father who art in heaven:
Let creation be still. Let all the people praise God together.

Hallowed be thy Name.
May thy holiness purge our hearts. In thy name we will take our stand.

Thy kingdom come.
Dawn upon this world of darkness with thy true light. Make all things new.

Thy will be done on earth as it is in heaven.
Open our minds and hearts to thy holy will. Free us from sin by the power of grace and love.

Give us this day our daily bread.
Free us as we labor in thy kingdom. Grant us the Bread of Heaven and the Water of Life which last forever.

Forgive us our debts as we forgive our debtors.
Deliver us from our worst selves. In the act of forgiving and receiving others may we know thy forgiveness of us.

Lead us not into temptation but deliver us from evil.
May the tests and trials of life not be more than we can bear.
For thine is the kingdom, the power, and the glory forever. Amen.

PAUL N. CONLEY
– WORSHIP SERVICES FOR SPECIAL OCCASIONS

•19 A Morning Litany

God, our Creator, you are the maker of heaven and earth:
Be our freedom, Lord!

God, our Savior, you redeem us all:
Be our freedom, Lord!

God, Holy Spirit, you sanctify our lives:
Be our freedom, Lord!

By your incarnation and your birth in poverty, by your baptism, your fasting, and your trials in the desert:
Be our freedom, Lord!

By your agony in the garden, by your cross and passion, by your death and burial, by your resurrection and ascension, and by the gifts of your Holy Spirit:
Be our freedom, Lord!

In times of trouble, and when all goes well, at the hour we die, and on the Day of your glory:
Be our freedom, Lord!

From war and violence, from hardness of heart and from contempt of your love and your promises:
Be our freedom, Lord!

Enlighten this day with your word, that in it we may find our way and our hope:
Be our freedom, Lord!

Assist your people in every land, govern them in peace and justice, defend them from the enemies of life:
Be our freedom, Lord!

PRAISE GOD: COMMON PRAYER AT TAIZÉ*

•20 At the Start of a New Day

In the morning,
I sing your praise, O Lord.

Lord, you have alwyas given me
tomorrow's bread:
And, although I am poor,
today I believe.

Lord, you have always mapped out
tomorrow's road:
And, although it is hidden,
today I believe.

Lord, you have always given me
tomorrow's peace:
And, in spite of my distress,
today I believe.

Lord, you have always given me
tomorrow's strength:
And, although I am weak,
today I believe.

Lord, you have always given me
tomorrow's light:
And, in spite of the darkness,
today I believe.

Lord, you have always spoken
when I was in doubt:
And, in spite of your silence,
today I believe.

Lord, you are my life;
you are my endless joy.
Even in death
forever I believe.

In the morning,
I sing your praise, O Lord. Amen.

LUCIEN DEISS*

From *Come, Lord Jesus,* © 1976, 1981 by Lucien Deiss. Reprinted with permission.

•21 Morning Suffrages

Show us your mercy, O Lord;
And grant us your salvation.

Clothe your ministers with righteousness;
Let your people sing with joy.

Give peace, O Lord, in all the world;
For only in you can we live in safety.

Lord, keep this nation under your care;
And guide us in the way of justice and truth.

Let your way be known upon earth;
Your saving health among all nations.

Let not the needy, O Lord, be forgotten;
Nor the hope of the poor be taken away.

Create in us clean hearts, O God;
And sustain us with your Holy Spirit.

THE BOOK OF COMMON PRAYER 1979*

•22 An Evening Litany

That this evening may be holy, good, and peaceful:
We entreat you, O Lord.

That your holy angels may lead us in paths of peace and goodwill:
We entreat you, O Lord.

That we may be pardoned and forgiven for our sins and offenses:
We entreat you, O Lord.

That there may be peace to your Church and to the whole world:
We entreat you, O Lord.

That we may depart this life in your faith and fear, and not be condemned before the great judgment seat of Christ:
We entreat you, O Lord.

That we may be bound together by your Holy Spirit in the communion of

[_____ and] all your saints, entrusting one another and all our life to Christ:
We entreat you, O Lord.

Silence

The Officiant then says one or more of the following Collects.

Lighten our darkness, we entreat you, O Lord; and in your great mercy
defend us from all perils and dangers of this night; for the love of your only
Son, our Savior, Jesus Christ. *Amen.*

O Lord God Almighty, as you have taught us to call the evening, the
morning, and the noonday one day; and have made the sun to know its going
down: Dispel the darkness of our hearts, that by your brightness we may
know you to be the true God and eternal light, living and reigning for ever
and ever. *Amen.*

Blessed are you, O Lord our God, creator of day and night, giving rest to
the weary and renewing the strength of those who are spent. As you have
protected us in the day that is past, so be with us in the coming night; keep
us from every sin, every evil, and every fear; for you are our light and
salvation, and the strength of our life. To you be glory for endless ages.
Amen.

Almighty, everlasting God, let our prayer in your sight be as incense, the
lifting up of our hands as the evening sacrifice. Give us grace to behold you,
present in your Word and Sacraments, and to recognize you in the lives of
those around us. Stir up in us the flame of that love which burned in the
heart of your Son as he bore his passion, and let it burn in us to eternal life
and to the ages of ages. *Amen.*

THE BOOK OF COMMON PRAYER 1979*

•23 At the End of the Day

Stay with us, Lord:
Behold, evening is coming,
and we still have not recognized your face
in each of our brothers and sisters.
Stay with us, Lord Jesus Christ.

Stay with us, Lord:
Behold, evening is coming,
and we still have not shared your bread
in thanksgiving with all our brothers and sisters.
Stay with us, Lord Jesus Christ.

Stay with us, Lord:
Behold, evening is coming,

and we still have not recognized your Word
in the words of all our brothers and sisters.
Stay with us, Lord Jesus Christ.

Stay with us, Lord:
Behold, evening is coming,
and our hearts are still too slow to believe
that you had to die in order to rise again.
Stay with us, Lord Jesus Christ.

Stay with us, Lord:
for our night itself becomes day
   when you are there!
Stay with us, Lord Jesus Christ.
Amen.

LUCIEN DEISS
From *Come, Lord Jesus,* © 1976, 1981 by Lucien Deiss.
Reprinted with permission.

• 24 For Those We Depend On

Heavenly Father: we pray today for the many people who serve us through
their work. Let us remember them.

Silence

We acknowledge in gratitude those who hallow their work by helpfulness:
   receptionists, secretaries, clerks, custodians;
   doctors, nurses, nurses' aides, surgeons, orderlies;
   chaplains, pastors, educators, postal clerks;
   judges, politicians, and delivery people.
Help them find joy in service, O Lord:
And give us gratitude and appreciation for all they do for us.

But work is not always satisfying. Let us remember those who do not enjoy
what they do.

Silence

We pray for
   people who are not suited to the jobs they are given;
   people caught in a web of dishonesty;
   people whose initiative is thwarted and who only follow orders;
   employers and employees who do not know how to relate to each other;
   people who feel they are victims of "the system";
   people who are too tired to do their best;
   people who exploit others.
Hear our prayers for them, O Lord:
And give us understanding and compassion in all we do for them.

Some work done for us each day is dangerous. Let us remember the men and women who protect our lives.

Silence

We pray for members of our Armed Forces;
for fire fighters and police and members of the Coast Guard;
for bus drivers, railroad engineers, jet pilots, and air traffic controllers;
for ambulance drivers and paramedics and rescue personnel.
Protect them and us in the face of danger, O Lord:
And give us all care and concern for each other's life and well-being. This we pray in Jesus' name. Amen.

MODELS FOR MINISTERS I*

•25 Our Many Communities

Father, you do not create us to live alone
and you have not made us all alike.
We thank you for the varied societies
into which we come,
by which we are brought up,
and through which we discover your purpose for our lives.
In gratitude we pray for our fellows.

This is my commandment:
Love one another, as I have loved you.

We pray for our families,
with whom we live day by day.
May this most searching test of our character
not find us broken and empty.
By all that we do and say
help us to build up the faith and confidence
of those we love,
and when we quarrel, help us to forgive quickly.

This is my commandment:
Love one another, as I have loved you.

We pray for the places where we work,
that there we may be workers who have no need to be ashamed.
We ask to be reliable rather than successful,
worthy of trust rather than popular.
Whether those we work with be many or few,
may we help to give them the sense that they are personally
wanted and cared for.

This is my commandment:

Love one another, as I have loved you.

We pray for the communities to which we belong,
  that we may be good citizens.
Make us willing to accept responsibility
    when we are called to it;
    make us willing also to give place to others,
      that they too may have their opportunity.
Grant that our influence may be good and not evil.

This is my commandment:
Love one another, as I have loved you.

We pray for the generation to which we belong,
  those with whom we share a common fund of memory,
    common standards of behavior
    and a common attitude toward the world.
Grant that the presence of Christ may be so real to us that we may be able to
  help our generation to see him also as our contemporary.

This is my commandment:
Love one another, as I have loved you.

Father, into whose world we come
    and from whose world finally we must go:
  we thank you for all those people,
    great and humble,
    who have maintained the fabric of the world's life in the past
    and left us a great inheritance.
May we take up and encourage what is good,
  and hand it on to those come after,
    believing that our work in your name will not be wasted or in vain.

This is my commandment:
Love one another, as I have loved you.
Amen.

CONTEMPORARY PRAYERS FOR PUBLIC WORSHIP

52

•26 For People of All Sorts and Conditions

O Blessed Trinity, One God,
Eternal friend to all your creation:
Inspire us with your love.

That there are people who hunger for warm rice,
Or milk, or meat, or cheese,
Or even the crumbs our dogs ignore:
Lord, help us to remember.

That there are people who hunger for your grace,
And search their minds and hearts for words of prayer,
Who, having your love, yet fail to find its presence:
Lord, help us to remember.

That there are people who hunger to be free,
To go where they please, or stay upon their land,
Or even to think, to laugh, to plan, to hope:
Lord, help us to remember.

That there are people who thirst to know the truth,
And have at hand some small, dry cup of lies
Provided them by cynical, evil leaders:
Lord, help us to remember.

That there are people who thirst to use themselves
In surging performance of all they have learned from life,
But are held back by the jealousy of their contemporaries:
Lord, help us to remember.

That there are people who thirst to create love
In loveless circumstance of slum and tenement,
Or homeless circumstance of refugee camp:
Lord, help us to remember.

That there are people who call their neighbor stranger,
Reject the world, and dwell within suspicion
In agonizing ignorance of their need for you:
Lord, help us to remember.

That there are people who, foreign to your Church,
Still seek you in the reaches of their hearts
And would come forth if they were gently asked:
Lord, help us to remember.

That there are people who, alien to themselves,
Become uneasy friends with fear,
Yet might with a moment's grace rejoice in knowledge of your love:
Lord, help us to remember.

That there are people naked to weather,
Helpless before torture,
Sick with disease and with loneliness,
That there are people prisoner to the walls of tyrants,
And prisoner to the walls of indifference,
That in the least of these your kingdom waits our love:
Lord, help us to remember.

Grant to us, O God,
A generous stewardship of self,
Possessions, and endeavor,
By hour, and by day,
By moment, and by night,
For the sake of him who came among us
To serve us all.
Lord, keep us in this faith which sustains people of all sorts and conditions.
Amen.

KAY SMALLZRIED

•27 For Compassion

O Savior of the world, by your cross and passion you have redeemed us:
Save us and help us, we entreat you, O Lord.

From the impatience that prevents us from discerning your purpose in pain
and sorrow:
Save us, good Lord.

From refusing to share the suffering of the world, from seeking only comfort
and pleasure, from forgetting those in distress, from the selfishness that
brings needless grief to others:
Save us, good Lord.

Almighty Father, in the afflictions of your people you are yourself afflicted;
hear us as we pray for those who suffer.

Silence

For all who are hindered in the race of life through no fault of their own;
for the defective and the delicate, and for those who are disabled:
We entreat you to hear us, good Lord.

For those whose livelihood is insecure; for the hungry, the homeless and
destitute; for those who are overworked, downtrodden, and in despair:
We entreat you to hear us, good Lord.

For little children whose surroundings hide from them your love and
beauty; for the fatherless and motherless, and for the unwanted:

We entreat you to hear us, good Lord.

For prisoners and captives, and all suffering from oppression:
We entreat you to hear us, good Lord.

For all who are suffering because of their faithfulness to conviction and duty:
We entreat you to hear us, good Lord.

For those who have to bear their burdens alone; for those who are in doubt
and anguish of soul; for those who are oversensitive, and for those who
suffer through their own wrongdoing:
We entreat you to hear us, good Lord.

For all who do not pray for themselves, and for all who have not the
consolation of the prayers of others, and for all whose anguish is unrelieved
by the knowledge of your love:
We entreat you to hear us, good Lord.

For the infirm and aged, and all who are growing weary with the journey of
life; and for all who are passing through the valley of death:
We entreat you to hear us, good Lord.

For all forgotten by us, but dear to you:
We entreat you to hear us, good Lord.

O God our Father, have regard to our prayers, answer them in your
compassion, and make us the channels of your infinite pity and helpfulness.
Amen.

DEVOTIONAL SERVICES FOR PUBLIC WORSHIP

Adoration and Praise

•28 Prayers of Adoration, Confession,
and Thanksgiving

*These prayers may be used separately or as one continuous litany. The hymn stanzas
may be said or sung, as desired.*

Stand

Adoration

Let us give glory to God: Father, Son, and Holy Spirit.
Let us pray.

Let us adore the God of love who created us;
who every moment preserves and sustains us;
who has loved us with an everlasting love, and given us the light of the
    knowledge of God's glory in the face of Jesus Christ.
We praise you, O God, we acknowledge you to be the Lord.

Let us glory in the grace of our Lord Jesus Christ;
who, though he was rich, yet for our sakes became poor;
who went about doing good and preaching the Gospel of the Kingdom;
who was tempted in all points like as we are, yet without sin;
who became obedient unto death, even the death of the Cross;
who was dead, and now lives for evermore;
who opened the Kingdom of Heaven to all believers;
who is seated at the right hand of God in the glory of the Father.
You are the King of Glory, O Christ.

Let us rejoice in the fellowship of the Holy Spirit, the Lord and Giver of
life, by whom we are born into the family of God, and made members of
the Body of Christ;
    whose witness confirms us;
    whose wisdom teaches us;

whose power enables us;
who waits to do for us exceeding abundantly
    above all that we ask or think.
All praise to you, O Holy Spirit.

Silence

The following hymn is said or sung.

You servants of God, your master proclaim,
and publish aborad his wonderful name;
the name, all-victorious, of Jesus extol;
his Kingdom is glorious and rules over all!

Then let us adore and give him his right,
all glory and pow'r and wisdom and might,
all honor and blessing, with angels above,
and thanks never ceasing, and infinite love!

Sit or kneel

Confession

Let us examine ourselves and humbly confess our sins before God.
Let us pray.

O God, you have set forth the way of life for us in your beloved Son: we
confess with shame our slowness to learn of him, our reluctance to follow
him. You have spoken and called, and we have not given heed; your beauty
has shone forth and we have been blind; you have stretched out your hands
to us through our fellows and we have passed by. We have taken great
benefits with little thanks; we have been unworthy of your changeless love.
Have mercy upon us and forgive us, O Lord.

Forgive us, we pray, the poverty of our worship, the formality and selfishness
of our prayers, our inconstancy and unbelief, our neglect of fellowship and of
the means of grace, our hesitating witness for Christ, our false pretenses and
our willful ignorance of your ways.
Have mercy upon us and forgive us, O Lord.

Forgive us wherein we have wasted our time or misused our gifts. Forgive us
wherein we have excused our own wrong-doing or evaded our
responsibilities. Forgive us that we have been unwilling to overcome evil
with good, that we have drawn back from the Cross.
Have mercy upon us and forgive us, O Lord.

Forgive us that so little of your love has reached others through us, and that
we have borne so lightly wrongs and sufferings that were not our own.
Forgive us wherein we have cherished the things that divide us from others,

and wherein we have made it hard for them to live with us. Forgive us wherein we have been thoughtless in judgment, hasty in condemnation, grudging in forgiveness.
Have mercy upon us and forgive us, O Lord.

If we have made no ventures in fellowship; if we have kept in our heart a grievance against another; if we have not sought reconciliation; if we have been eager for the punishment of wrong-doers, and slow to seek their redemption:
Have mercy upon us and forgive us, O Lord.

Silence

The following hymn is said or sung.

Come, O thou all-victorious Lord,	*Give us ourselves and thee to know,*
thy pow'r to us make known;	*in this our gracious day;*
strike with the hammer of thy Word,	*repentance unto life bestow,*
and break these hearts of stone.	*and take our sins away.*

Stand

Thanksgiving

Let us give thanks to God for all the blessings of our life in Christ.
Let us pray.

O God, the fountain of all goodness, you have been gracious to us through all the years of our life: we give you thanks for your loving-kindness which has filled our days and brought us to this time and place.
We praise your holy Name, O Lord.

You have given us life and reason and set us in a world which is full of your glory. You have comforted us with family and friends, and ministered to us through the hands and minds of our fellows.
We praise your holy Name, O Lord.

You have set in our hearts a hunger for you, and given us your peace. You have redeemed us and called us to a high calling in Christ Jesus. You have given us a place in the fellowship of your Spirit and the witness of your Church.
We praise your holy Name, O Lord.

In darkness you have been our light; in adversity and temptation a rock of strength; in our joys the very spirit of joy; in our labors the all-sufficient reward.
We praise your holy Name, O Lord.

You have remembered us when we have forgotten you, followed us even when we fled from you, met us with forgiveness when we turned back to you. For all your long-suffering and the abundance of your grace: *We praise your holy Name, O Lord.*

Silence

The following hymn is said or sung.

O, for a thousand tongues to sing my great Redeemer's praise, the glories of my God and King, the triumphs of his grace!

My gracious Master and my God, assist me to proclaim, to spread through all the earth abroad the honors of thy name.

JOHN WESLEY'S COVENANT SERVICE
– HYMN STANZAS BY CHARLES WESLEY*

•29 Short Litany of the Holy Trinity

I glorify you, most holy Trinity, with my spirit, my soul, and my body.

Blessed be the holy and undivided Trinity,
Now and henceforth and for ever and ever. Amen.

Grant, O Lord, that I may give you choice gifts, three sweet-smelling perfumes, three lighted and dazzling torches.
To the Father, and the Son, and the Holy Ghost.

My spirit to the Father, my soul to the Son, my body to the Holy Ghost who will renew it from the dust of the grave.
To the Father, and the Son, and the Holy Ghost.

O Father, who created me, sanctify my spirit, that I may be sheltered from temptation by the wings of your protection.
Eternal Wisdom, sanctify my spirit.

Give me intelligence, O Lord, and increase my understanding.
Eternal Wisdom, sanctify my spirit.

O Son, who redeemed me, sanctify my soul, that I may be more pleasing to you than the sweet smell of incense.
Divine Word, sanctify my soul.

That I may love you and hate the corruption in the world; that I may cling to you rather than to the things which pass away.
Divine Word, sanctify my soul.

O Holy Ghost, who made my body your temple, watch over my eyes that
they look not upon evil, my ears that they hear no wickedness.
Indwelling Spirit, sanctify my body.

Bridle my mouth and my lips that they speak no ill; stand guard over my
heart lest it be moved to sin.
Indwelling Spirit, sanctify my body.

Grant, O Lord, that I may rejoice in you now and laugh on the day of
judgment.
May your mercy be ever upon me. Amen.

Blessed be the holy and undivided Trinity,
Now and henceforth and for ever and ever. Amen.

I glorify you, most holy Trinity, with my spirit, my soul, and my body.

ADAPTED BY BENJAMIN F. MUSSER
FROM A PRAYER IN THE MARONITE RITE

•30 A Song of Creation

*One or more sections of this Canticle may be used. Whatever the selection, it begins
with the Invocation and concludes with the Doxology.*

Invocation

Glorify the Lord, all you works of the Lord:
Praise God and highly exalt him for ever.
In the firmament of his power, glorify the Lord:
Praise God and highly exalt him for ever.

I. The Cosmic Order

Glorify the Lord, you angels and all powers of the Lord:
O heavens and all waters above the heavens.
Sun and moon and stars of the sky, glorify the Lord:
Praise God and highly exalt him for ever.

Glorify the Lord, every shower of rain and fall of dew:
All winds and fire and heat.
Winter and summer, glorify the Lord:
Praise God and highly exalt him for ever.

Glorify the Lord, O chill and cold:
Drops of dew and flakes of snow.
Frost and cold, ice and sleet, glorify the Lord:

Praise God and highly exalt him for ever.

Glorify the Lord, O nights and days:
O shining light and enfolding dark.
Storm clouds and thunderbolts, glorify the Lord:
Praise God and highly exalt him for ever.

II. The Earth and Its Creatures

Let the earth glorify the Lord:
Praise God and highly exalt him for ever.
Glorify the Lord, O mountains and hills,
and all that grows upon the earth:
Praise God and highly exalt him for ever.

Glorify the Lord, O springs of water, seas, and streams:
O whales and all that move in the waters.
All the birds of the air, glorify the Lord:
Praise God and highly exalt him for ever.

Glorify the Lord, O beasts of the wild:
And all you flocks and herds.
O men and women everywhere, glorify the Lord:
Praise God and highly exalt him for ever.

III. The People of God

Let the people of God glorify the Lord:
Praise God and highly exalt him for ever.
Glorify the Lord, O priests and servants of the Lord:
Praise God and highly exalt him for ever.

Glorify the Lord, O spirits and souls of the righteous:
Praise God and highly exalt him for ever.
You that are holy and humble of heart, glorify the Lord:
Praise God and highly exalt him for ever.

Doxology

Let us glorify the Lord: Father, Son, and Holy Spirit:
Praise God and highly exalt him for ever.
In the firmament of his power, glorify the Lord:
Praise God and highly exalt him for ever.

THE BOOK OF COMMON PRAYER 1979*

• 31 Litany of Praises

Three voices may lead this.

I   Alleluia!
      O give thanks to the Lord for he is good,
II   Give thanks to the God of gods,
III Give thanks to the Lord of lords:
      Great is his love, love without end.

I   Who alone has wrought marvelous works,
II   Whose wisdom it was made the skies,
III Who fixed the earth firmly on the seas:
      Great is his love, love without end.

I   It was he who made the great lights,
II   The sun to rule in the day,
III The moon and stars in the night:
      Great is his love, love without end.

I   The first-born of the Egyptians he smote,
II   He brought Israel out from their midst,
II   Arm outstretched, with power in his hand:
      Great is his love, love without end.

I   He divided the Red Sea in two,
II   He made Israel pass through the midst,
III He flung Pharaoh and his force in the sea:
      Great is his love, love without end.

I   Through the desert his people he led,
II   Nations in their greatness he struck,
III Kings in their splendor he slew:
      Great is his love, love without end.

I   Sihon, King of the Amorites,
      and Og, the king of Bashan,
II   He let Israel inherit their land,
III On his servant their land he bestowed:
      Great is his love, love without end.

I   He remembered us in our distress,
II   And he snatched us away from our foes;
III He gives food to all living things:
      Great is his love, love without end.

I, II To the God of heaven give thanks:
III   *Great is his love, love without end. Amen.*

PSALM 136
–THE PSALMS: A NEW TRANSLATION*

•32 The Gracious Acts of God

People of God, let us praise the Lord.
With one voice we give thanks and praise to God!

God made the world, and out of that world called forth growth. God raised up the mountains and carved out the seas. God unmasked the dark and made the light shine in his world. God created us, man and woman, in his own image.
For the glory of creation we give thanks and praise to God!

God made a gracious covenant with Abraham, Isaac, and Jacob, and when we became enslaved, called us out of our bondage. When we turned our backs on him, God loved us and led us, as a child, on a holy pilgrimage.
For the certainty of God's promises, and for God's hand in our deliverance, we give thanks and praise to God!

In the night of our rebellion God put his judgment over us, and in the dawn of our brokenness God came to us in mercy.
For the prophets and for God's forgiving love, we give thanks and praise to God!

When we were oppressed by our own blindness, God came to us as a brother and gave us sight. God suffered with us and for us so that we might have his peace.
For God's presence through Jesus Christ, we give thanks and praise to God!

God called us together in his name and baptized us into a new people, remembering his promises to our ancestors. God showed us how to bear one another's burdens, and how to find healing through his presence among us.
For the gift of God's Church, we give thanks and praise to God!

God continues to create, to liberate, to judge, to love, to suffer, and to give peace – so that God's name might be glorified and so that we might have life more abundantly.
For all God's gifts, we give thanks and praise to God!
Amen.

UNION THEOLOGICAL SEMINARY*

•33 The God of Our Mothers

A wandering Aramean was my mother.
In Egypt she bore slaves.
Then she called to the God of our mothers.
Sarah, Hagar, Rebeccah, Rachel, Leah.
Praise God who hears, forever.

A warrior, judge, and harlot was my mother.
God used her from time to time.
She gave what she gave, and was willing.
Rahab, Jael, Deborah, Judith, Tamar.
Praise God who takes, forever.

A Galilean virgin was my mother.
She bore our Life and Hope.
And a sword pierced her own soul, also.
Mary, blessed among women, mother of God.
Praise God who loves, forever.

A witness to Christ's rising was my mother.
What angels said, she told.
The apostles thought it was an idle tale.
Mary, Mary Magdalene, Joanna, women with them.
Praise God who lives, forever.

A faithful Christian woman was my mother.
A mystic. Martyr. Saint.
May we, with her, in every generation,
Julian, Perpetua, Clare, Hilda, _____:
Praise God who made us,
Praise God who saved us,
Praise God who keeps us all, forever.
Amen.

MARTHA BLACKLOCK*

•34 Glory to God and to the Lamb

Lord God our Father,
most wonderful, most gracious, most glorious God,
we praise and adore you for all that you have done for us in Jesus Christ.

Though the divine nature was his from the first,
yet he did not think to snatch at equality with you,

but made himself nothing, assuming the nature of a slave:
Father, we lift up our hearts:
And bring you our worship and praise.

Bearing the human likeness, revealed in human shape,
he humbled himself, and in obedience accepted even death,
death on a cross:
Father, we lift up our hearts:
And bring you our worship and praise.

Therefore you raised him to the heights, and bestowed on him the name
above all names,
that at the name of Jesus every knee should bow,
in heaven, on earth, and in the depths,
and every tongue confess that he is Lord:
Father, we lift up our hearts:
And bring you our worship and praise.

Worthy is the Lamb that was slain to receive all power and wealth,
wisdom and might, honor and glory and praise!
Praise and honor, glory and might, to God who sits on the throne,
and to the Lamb, for ever and ever.
Praise God, from whom all blessings flow;
Praise God, all creatures here below;
Praise God above, ye heav'nly host:
Praise Father, Son, and Holy Ghost.
Amen.

CONTEMPORARY PRAYERS FOR PUBLIC WORSHIP*

•35 The Mercy of God

Lord, have mercy on us.
Christ, have mercy on us.
Lord, have mercy on us.

Christ, hear us.
Christ, graciously hear us.

God the Father of heaven, *have mercy on us.*
God the Son, Redeemer of the world, *have mercy on us.*
God the Holy Ghost, *have mercy on us.*
Holy Trinity, one God, *have mercy on us.*

The Response: "In this we put our trust."

Mercy of God, supreme attribute of the Creator: *(Response)*
Mercy of God, greatest gift of the Redeemer:
Mercy of God, unfathomable love of the Sanctifier:
Mercy of God, summoning us to existence out of nothingness:
Mercy of God, embracing the whole universe:
Mercy of God, bestowing upon us eternal life:
Mercy of God, shielding us from punishment:
Mercy of God, raising us from the misery of sin:
Mercy of God, justifying us in the Word Incarnate:
Mercy of God, flowing from the wounds of Christ:
Mercy of God, manifested in the founding of the Church:
Mercy of God, revealed in the institution of the Sacraments:
Mercy of God, bestowed upon us in Baptism:
Mercy of God, granted to us at every Eucharist:
Mercy of God, shown in calling us to Faith:
Mercy of God, revealed in the conversion of sinners:
Mercy of God, fulfilled in the perfecting of the saintly:
Mercy of God, fount of health for the sick and suffering:
Mercy of God, solace of anguished hearts:
Mercy of God, hope of souls afflicted with despair:
Mercy of God, always and everywhere accompanying your people:
Mercy of God, going before us with grace:
Mercy of God, peace of the dying:
Mercy of God, heavenly delight of the blessed:
Mercy of God, crown of all the saints:

Lamb of God, you showed your greatest mercy in redeeming the world on the Cross.
Spare us, O Lord.

Lamb of God, you take away the sins of the world.
Have mercy on us.

Lord, have mercy on us.
Christ, have mercy on us.
Lord, have mercy on us.

The tender mercies of the Lord are over all his works.
The mercies ofthe Lord I will sing for ever.

Let us pray.

O God, your mercy is infinite and your pity inexhaustible; graciously look down on us and increase in us mercy so that we may never, even in our greatest trials, give way to despair, but may always trustfully conform ourselves to your holy will, which is mercy itself; through our Lord Jesus

Christ, the King of mercy, who, with you and the Holy Ghost, shows us mercy for ever and ever. *Amen.*

MICHAEL SOPOCKO
–TRANSLATED BY THE MARIAN FATHERS*

• 36 A Litany of Praise

Spirit of God, the fountain of beauty and goodness, from whom stream all things excellent in life and nature, open our eyes to see your wonder-working in the world and to rejoice in you.
Bless the Lord, O my soul,
and forget not all God's benefits.

For the constancy and beauty of creation; for the breath of winds, the scent of flowers, the racing clouds, the glory of the trees; for the procession of days and nights, the rhythm of seasons, and the wonder of stars:
Bless the Lord, O my soul,
and forget not all God's benefits.

For all beauty in human thought and deed, for poet's song and prophet's word, the gift of music and the grace of art; for nobility of character, for the loveliness of friendship, and for the fragrance of souls nourished in peace:
Bless the Lord, O my soul,
and forget not all God's benefits.

Calm our too easily disquieted spirits that they may reflect your presence in all things excellent and of good report; take the dimness of our souls away. Free our hearts from lethargy, our spirits from discouragement, and our lips from complaining, that we may rejoice in you.
Bless the Lord, O my soul,
and forget not all God's benefits.

For every inward intimation that we are your children; for hours of insight when we have clearly seen your living presence and have been persuaded of your love; for that we cannot live by bread alone nor find rest until we rest in you:
Bless the Lord, O my soul,
and forget not all God's benefits.

For all victories of good over evil, wisdom over ignorance, love over hate, we praise you. For ancient superstitions overpassed and ancient oppressions done away; for the evident working of your purpose in the breaking of

67

bondage, the enlargement of opportunity, the victories of peace, and the diffusion of light:
Bless the Lord, O my soul,
and forget not all God's benefits.

For courage to endure hazard and hardship we praise you. For the tutelage of your Spirit teaching us how trials are to be borne and with what answer they are to be beaten back; for spiritual valor to face life's adventure, neither seducing others, nor ourselves seduced by fear; for strength to do what is appointed and for faith to leave the unsolved mysteries in your care:
Bless the Lord, O my soul,
and forget not all God's benefits.

May all our living speak your praise. By faithful work and wholesome leisure, by daily kindliness, by truthfulness of life and tongue, by secret living in your sight and outward service for the good of all:
Bless the Lord, O my soul,
and forget not all God's benefits.
Amen.

HARRY EMERSON FOSDICK

• 37 Sing a New Song to the Lord

O sing a new song to the Lord: sing to the Lord, all the earth.
O sing to the Lord, bless his name: proclaim his help day by day.
Give the Lord, you families of peoples,
　　Give the Lord glory and power:
　　Give the Lord the glory of his name.

It is the Lord who has brought us together to pray, and praise, and receive instruction.
　　Give the Lord glory and power:
　　Give the Lord the glory of his name.

It is the Lord who has shown his great love for us,
and has taught us, through Christ, to call him "Father."
　　Give the Lord glory and power:
　　Give the Lord the glory of his name.

It is the Lord who gives us strength to do our work and earn our living, and leisure to enjoy the results of our work.
　　Give the Lord glory and power:
　　Give the Lord the glory of his name.

68

It is the Lord who enables us to harness the world's resources
to provide warmth, and power, and machines to reduce life's drudgery.
Give the Lord glory and power:
Give the Lord the glory of his name.

It is the Lord who enlarges our vision by the work of artists and craftsmen,
and the deeds of courageous men and women.
Give the Lord glory and power:
Give the Lord the glory of his name.

Holy, holy, holy Lord, God of power and might,
heaven and earth are full of your glory.
Hosanna in the highest.

CONTEMPORARY PRAYERS FOR PUBLIC WORSHIP

•38 Alleluia, Alleluia

Two voices may lead this:

I: Alleluia!
    Sing to the Lord a new song;
    sing God's praise in the congregation of the faithful.
II: Let Israel rejoice in its Maker;
    let the children of Zion be joyful in their King.
    When in our music God is glorified,
    and adoration leaves no room for pride,
    it is as though the whole creation cried:
    Alleluia!

I: Let them praise God's Name in the dance;
    let them sing praise to God with timbrel and harp.
II: For the Lord takes pleasure in his people
    and adorns the poor with victory.
    How often, making music, we have found
    a new dimension in the world of sound,
    as worship moved us to a more profound
    Alleluia!

I: Alleluia!
    Praise God in his holy temple;
    praise God in the firmament of his power.

II: Praise God for his mighty acts;
praise God for his excellent greatness.
So has the Church, in liturgy and song,
in faith and love, through centuries of wrong,
borne witness to the truth in ev'ry tongue:
Alleluia!

I: Praise God with the blast of the ram's-horn;
praise God with lyre and harp.
II: Praise God with timbrel and dance;
praise God with strings and pipe.
And did not Jesus sing a psalm that night
when utmost evil strove against the Light?
Then let us sing, for whom he won the fight:
Alleluia!

I: Praise God with resounding cymbals;
praise God with loud-clanging cymbals.
II: Let everything that has breath praise the Lord.
Alleluia!
Let ev'ry instrument be tuned for praise;
let all rejoice who have a voice to raise;
and may God give us faith to sing always:
Alleluia!

THE BOOK OF COMMON PRAYER 1979
–HYMN STANZAS BY F. PRATT GREEN*

Confession

• 39 The Ten Commandments and Our Lord's Summary of the Law

Our Lord Jesus Christ said, If you love me, keep my commandments;
happy are those who hear the word of God and keep it. Hear then these
commandments which God has given to his people, and take them to heart.

I am the Lord your God: you shall have no other gods but me.
You shall love the Lord your God with all your heart, with all your soul,
with all your mind and with all your strength.
Amen. Lord, have mercy.

You shall not make for yourself any idol.
God is spirit, and those who worship God must worship in spirit and in
truth.
Amen. Lord, have mercy.

You shall not dishonor the name of the Lord your God.
You shall worship God with awe and reverence.
Amen. Lord, have mercy.

Remember the Lord's day and keep it holy.
Christ is risen from the dead: set your minds on things that are above,
not on things that are on the earth.
Amen. Lord, have mercy.

Honor your father and mother.
Live as servants of God; honor all people; love your brothers and sisters in
Christ.
Amen. Lord, have mercy.

You shall not commit murder.
Be reconciled to each other; overcome evil with good.
Amen. Lord, have mercy.

You shall not commit adultery.
Know that your body is a temple of the Holy Spirit.
Amen. Lord, have mercy.

You shall not steal.
Be honest in all that you do and care for those in need.
Amen. Lord, have mercy.

You shall not be a false witness.
Let everyone speak the truth.
Amen. Lord, have mercy.

You shall not covet anything which belongs to your neighbor.
Remember the words of the Lord Jesus: It is more blessed to give than to
receive. Love your neighbor as yourself, for love is the fulfilling of the law.
Amen. Lord, have mercy.

Our Lord Jesus Christ said: The first commandment is this: "Hear, O Israel,
the Lord our God is the only Lord. You shall love the Lord your God with
all your heart, with all your soul, with all your mind, and with all your
strength." The second is this: "Love your neighbor as yourself." There is no
other commandment greater than these.
Amen. Lord, have mercy.

THE ALTERNATIVE SERVICE BOOK 1980*

•40 Litany of the Commandments

The Law was given through Moses.
Grace and truth came through Jesus Christ.

I am the Lord your God, who brought you out of the land of Egypt, out of
the house of bondage: you shall have no other gods before me.
No one can serve two masters: you cannot serve God and mammon.

You shall not make yourself any graven images: for I, the Lord, am a
jealous God.
*Render therefore to Caesar the things that are Caesar's, and to God the things
that are God's.*

You shall not take the name of the Lord your God in vain.
*Let what you say be simply "Yes" or "No"; anything more than this comes
from the Evil One.*

Remember the Sabbath day to keep it holy.

The Sabbath was made for man, not man for the Sabbath: and the Son of man is Lord even of the Sabbath.

Honor your father and your mother, that your days be long in the land which the Lord your God gives you.
Who is my mother? Who are my brothers? Whoever does the will of my Father in heaven is my brother, and sister, and mother.

You shall not kill.
Love your enemies. Pray for those who persecute you. For if you love those who love you, what reward have you?

You shall not commit adultery.
Woman, has no one condemned you? Neither do I condemn you. Go, and sin no more.

You shall not steal.
Go, sell what you possess, and give to the poor, and you will have treasure in heaven.

You shall not bear false witness against your neighbor.
When it was evening, Jesus sat at table with the twelve disciples, and as they were eating, he said, "Truly, I say to you, one of you will betray me."

You shall not covet.
This is my body broken for you. This is my blood of the new covenant, which is poured out for many, for the forgiveness of sins.

The Law was given through Moses.
Grace and truth came through Jesus Christ.
Amen.

MODELS FOR MINISTERS I*

•41 Confession of the Community

O Lord, you open your hand, and all the earth is filled with good things, but we have cried out against you, saying, "What shall we eat and what shall be drink?"

Men: *Lord, have mercy upon us.*
Women: *Christ, have mercy upon us.*
All: *Lord, have mercy upon us.*

O Lord, you have said, "In returning and rest you shall be saved; in quietness and trust shall be your strength," but we have shouted, "No! We will speed upon horses, we will ride upon swift steeds."

Men: *Lord, have mercy upon us.*
Women: *Christ, have mercy upon us.*
All: *Lord, have mercy upon us.*

O Lord, you have said, "Let justice roll down like waters, and righteousness like an everflowing stream," but we have said, "When will the Sabbath be over that we may buy the poor for silver and the needy for a pair of sandals?"

Men: *Lord, have mercy upon us.*
Women: *Christ, have mercy upon us.*
All: *Lord, have mercy upon us.*

O Lord, we have come before you with thousands of rams and ten thousand rivers of oil, and we have caused you to cry out, "Oh my people, what have I done to you? In what have I wearied you? Answer me!"

Men: *Lord, have mercy upon us.*
Women: *Christ, have mercy upon us.*
All: *Lord, have mercy upon us.*

O Lord, you have said, "How can I give you up, O Ephriam? How can I hand you over, O Israel?" but we have cried out, "Away with him, away with him! We have no king but Caesar!"

Men: *Lord, have mercy upon us.*
Women: *Christ, have mercy upon us.*
All: *Lord, have mercy upon us.*

KATHERINE MEYER CAFOLLA*

• 42 Litany for Days of Penitence

The response after each line is "Our Father, our King!"

Our Father, our King! we have sinned before thee. *(Response)*
Our Father, our King! we have no king but thee.
Our Father, our King! deal with us for the sake of thy Name.
Our Father, our King! let a happy year begin for us.
Our Father, our King! nullify all evil decrees against us.
Our Father, our King! nullify the designs of those that hate us.
Our Father, our King! make the counsel of our enemies of none effect.
Our Father, our King! rid us of every oppressor and adversary.
Our Father, our King! close the mouths of our adversaries and accusers.

Our Father, our King! of pestilence and the sword, of famine, captivity and destruction, rid the children of thy covenant.

Our Father, our King! withhold the plague from thine inheritance.

Our Father, our King! forgive and pardon all our iniquities.

Our Father, our King! blot out our transgressions, and make them pass away from before thine eyes.

Our Father, our King! erase in thine abundant memories all the records of our guilt.

Our Father, our King! bring us back in perfect repentance unto thee.

Our Father, our King! send a perfect healing to the sick of thy people.

Our Father, our King! rend the evil judgment decreed against us.

Our Father, our King! let thy remembrance of us be for good.

Our Father, our King! inscribe us in the book of happy life.

Our Father, our King! inscribe us in the book of redemption and salvation.

Our Father, our King! inscribe us in the book of maintenance and sustenance.

Our Father, our King! inscribe us in the book of merit.

Our Father, our King! inscribe us in the book of forgiveness and pardon.

Our Father, our King! let salvation soon spring forth for us.

Our Father, our King! raise up the strength of Israel, thy people.

Our Father, our King! raise up the strength of thine anointed.

Our Father, our King! fill our hands with thy blessings.

Our Father, our King! fill our storehouses with plenty.

Our Father, our King! hear our voice, spare us, and have mercy upon us.

Our Father, our King! receive our prayer in mercy and in favor.

Our Father, our King! open the gates of heaven unto our prayer.

Our Father, our King! we pray thee, turn us not back empty from thy presence.

Our Father, our King! remember that we are but dust.

Our Father, our King! let this hour be an hour of mercy and a time of favor with thee.

Our Father, our King! have compassion upon us and upon our children and our infants.

Our Father, our King! do this for the sake of them that were slain for thy holy Name.

Our Father, our King! do it for the sake of them that were slaughtered for thy Unity.

Our Father, our King! do it for the sake of them that went
through fire and water for the sanctification of thy Name.
Our Father, our King! avenge before our eyes the blood of thy
servants that hath been shed.
Our Father, our King! do it for thy sake, if not for ours.
Our Father, our King! do it for thy sake, and save us.
Our Father, our King! do it for the sake of thine abundant
mercies.
Our Father, our King! do it for the sake of thy great, mighty
and revered Name by which we are called.
Our Father, our King! be gracious unto us and answer us, for
we have no good works of our own; deal with us in charity and kindness,
and save us.

THE AUTHORIZED DAILY PRAYER BOOK*

•43 We're Sorry, God

That we don't think much about you:
We're sorry, God.

That we use your name cheaply:
We're sorry, God.

That we make believe we don't care about you:
We're sorry, God.

That we think it's big to be like that:
We're sorry, God.

That we poke fun at people who go to church:
We're sorry, God.

That we've waited so long to say we're sorry:
We're sorry, God.

That we've caused you pain:
We're sorry, God.

That we forget your love:
We're sorry, God.

For showing off and making fools of ourselves:
We're sorry, God.

For not finding out about you:
We're sorry, God.

For fighting you:
We're sorry, God.

For not trusting you:
We're sorry, God.

For thinking we are all alone:
We're sorry, God.

For the times we've said, "Who needs God?"
We're sorry, God.

For all that sort of thing:
We're sorry, God.
Amen:

CARL F. BURKE

•44 A Cry from the Heart

With the tax-collector in St. Luke's Gospel, let us say:
O God, be merciful to me, a sinner.

You come to look for the lost sheep;
joyfully you carry it on your shoulders–
     we beg you:
O God, be merciful to me, a sinner.

You go to meet the prodigal son;
you clasp him in your arms and kiss him–
     we beg you:
O God, be merciful to me, a sinner.

You choose, as your apostle, Matthew the tax-collector;
you have not come to call the righteous, but sinners–
     we beg you:
O God, be merciful to me, a sinner.

You enter the house of Zachaeus the tax-gatherer
in order to seek out and save what was lost–
     we beg you:
O God, be merciful to me, a sinner.

You accept the ointment of the sinful woman;
because of her tears you pardon and defend her–
     we beg you:
O God, be merciful to me, a sinner.

To the good thief who implores you,
you open the gate of Paradise–
   we beg you:
O God, be merciful to me, a sinner.
Amen.

LUCIEN DIESS

From *Come, Lord Jesus,* © 1976, 1981 by Lucien Deiss. Reprinted with permission.

•45 A Litany of Confession

O God our Father, we want to remember Jesus. Especially we want to remember how he went into a quiet place to think and pray and choose what he would do. Help us to bring our minds and hearts, as he brought his, for you to see. We are not like him, who had nothing to be ashamed of; but we want to be like him, as much as we can. We are sorry for anything in us that is wrong, and we pray for a blessing on everything in us that is good; for Jesus' sake. *Amen.*

If we are to do better today and tomorrow, we need to be forgiven for the blunders we have already made. And so, for all our faults we know of, and for the mistakes we made because we did not know:
We ask forgiveness.

For greediness or laziness, and for anything that has kept our bodies from being at their best:
Forgive us, O God.

For not trying hard enough to find out what was right, and for cowardice in not standing up for what we knew was right and true:
Forgive us.

For thinking so much about ourselves that we did not think of others and of what we might do for them:
Forgive us.

For trying to get the best things for ourselves instead of being quick to make sure that others had their share:
Forgive us.

For the times when we have hurt anybody, and for the times when we have been too careless to be kind:
Forgive us.

For the hasty words our tongues have spoken, and for the helpful words we did not have the sense to say:
Forgive us.

For any unclean speech or cruel gossip, and for ever forgetting to repeat the good things which would have made somebody glad:
Forgive us.

For any lies we may have told, and for the other lies we helped to spread by keeping silence when the truth was twisted:
Forgive us.

For ever having bullied those who are not as big as we, or having shared in making someone else unhappy:
Forgive us.

For being bad-tempered or depressed, and for nursing our grievances when we ought to have gone ahead cheerfully:
Forgive us.

For cheating or crookedness in work or play or sport, and for cutting corners to get the things we wanted:
Forgive us.

For the rudenesses which have disappointed those who loved us, and for every chance we have lost to be courteous and kind:
Forgive us.

But we do not ask, dear God, to be forgiven only. We want to be better than we have been before.
We remember Jesus, who gave his body, mind, and soul for God to use.
Help us to follow him.

By his shining goodness, he can make us glad in being good.
Help us to follow him.

By his strength he can make us strong.
Help us to follow him.

By his bravery he can make us brave.
Help us to follow him.

By his truth he can keep us true.
Help us to follow him.

And so, Father, as we have asked for blessing in our worship, we ask again for blessing as we go away. Help us to remember all that we have prayed for, and to trust in you to answer all our prayers; for Jesus' sake. *Amen.*

WALTER RUSSELL BOWIE

•46 The *Godspell* Confession

Two voices may lead this.

I: Father, hear thy children's call;
    Humbly at thy feet we fall,
    Prodigals, confessing all:
    We beseech thee, hear us.

II: Love, that caused us first to be,
    Love, that bled upon the tree,
    Love, that draws us lovingly:
    We beseech thee, hear us.

I: We thy call have disobeyed,
    Into paths of sin have strayed,
    And repentance have delayed:
    We beseech thee, hear us.

II: Sick, we come to thee for cure,
    Guilty, seek thy mercy sure,
    Evil, long to be made pure:
    We beseech thee, hear us.

I: Blind, we pray that we may see;
    Bound, we pray to be made free;
    Stained, we pray for sanctity:
    We beseech thee, hear us.

II: By the gracious saving call,
    Spoken tenderly to all,
    Sharing Adam's guilt and fall:
    We beseech thee, hear us.

I: By the love that longs to bless,
    Pitying our sore distress,
    Leading us to holiness:
    We beseech thee, hear us.

II: By the love so calm and strong,
    Patient still to suffer wrong,
    And our day of grace prolong:
    We beseech thee, hear us.

I: By the love that speaks within,
    Calling us to flee from sin,
    And the joy of goodness win:
    We beseech thee, hear us.

II: Teach us what thy love has borne,
    That, with loving sorrow torn,
    Truly contrite we may mourn:
    We beseech thee, hear us.

I: Grant us faith to know thee near,
    Hail thy grace, thy judgment fear,
    And through trails persevere:
    We beseech thee, hear us.

II: Grant us hope from earth to rise,
    And to strain with eager eyes,
    T'wards the promised heav'nly prize:
    We beseech thee, hear us.

I: Grant us love, thy love to own,
    Love to live for thee alone,
    And the power of grace make known:
    We beseech thee, hear us.

II: Lead us daily nearer thee,
    Till at last thy face we see,
    Crowned with thine own purity:
    We beseech thee, hear us.

THOMAS BENSON POLLOCK
–USED IN PART IN GODSPELL*

Thanksgiving

• 47 Litany of Thanksgiving

Give thanks to the Lord, for God is good.
God's love is everlasting.

Come, let us praise God joyfully.
Let us come to God with thanksgiving.

For the good world; for things great and small, beautiful and awesome; for seen and unseen splendors:
Thank you, God.

For human life; for talking and moving and thinking together; for common hopes and hardships shared from birth until our dying:
Thank you, God.

For work to do and strength to work; for the comradeship of labor; for exchanges of good humor and encouragement:
Thank you, God.

For marriage; for the mystery and joy of flesh made one; for mutual forgiveness and burdens shared; for secrets kept in love:
Thank you, God.

For family; for living together and eating together; for family amusements and family pleasures:
Thank you, God.

For children; for their energy and curiosity; for their brave play and their startling frankness; for their sudden sympathies:
Thank you, God.

For the young; for their high hopes; for their irreverence toward worn-out values; their search for freedom; their solemn vows:
Thank you, God.

For growing up and growing old; for wisdom deepened by experience; for rest in leisure; and for time made precious by its passing:
Thank you, God.

For your help in times of doubt and sorrow; for healing our diseases; for preserving us in temptation and danger:
Thank you, God.

For the Church into which we have been called; for the good news we receive by Word and Sacrament; for our life together in the Lord:
We praise you, God.

For your Holy Spirit, who guides our steps and brings us gifts of faith and love; who prays in us and prompts our grateful worship:
We praise you, God.

Above all, O God, for your Son Jesus Christ, who lived and died and lives again for our salvation; for our hope in him; and for the joy of serving him:
We thank and praise you, God our Father, for all your goodness to us.

Give thanks to the Lord, for God is good.
God's love is everlasting. Amen.

THE WORSHIPBOOK

•48 Thanksgiving at the Start of the Day

For flowers that bloom about our feet:
Father, we thank you;

For tender grass so fresh and sweet:
Father, we thank you;

For song of bird and hum of bee,
For all things fair we hear or see:
Father in heaven, we thank you.

For blue of stream and blue of sky:
Father, we thank you;

For pleasant shade of branches high:
Father, we thank you;

For fragrant air and cooling breeze,
For beauty of the blooming trees:
Father in heaven, we thank you.

For this new morning with its light:

Father, we thank you;

For rest and shelter of the night:
Father, we thank you;

For health and food, for love and friends,
For everything your goodness sends:
Father in heaven, we thank you. Amen.

RALPH WALDO EMERSON
–TABLE PRAYERS

•49 A Counting of Blessings

O God: we thank you for morning light:
And evening peace;

For the night in which you restore our spirit's strength:
And the day in which you lead us into larger life;

For the past, from which so much has come to bless us:
And for the future, to which we lift our eyes in hope;

For the body in which our souls are nurtured:
And for the soul by which our body is glorified;

For the mind which asks the probing questions:
And the spirit by which life's mysteries are exalted;

For truth which binds the conscience in law:
And the mercy which frees it from bondage;

For beauty that rejoices the eye:
And for the skill that disciplines the hand;

For the saints whose deeds and dreams are one:
*And for the sinners who hunger and thirst beyond their deeds for
benediction;*

For love that redeems the heart from fear:
And for grace that sustains us in every adversity.

*For all your work done in this world,
we give you thanks, O God,
our Strength and our Redeemer. Amen.*

SAMUEL H. MILLER
–MODELS FOR MINISTERS I*

•50 God's Saving Work

We give you thanks, O God, for revealing your power in the creation of the universe, and for your providence in the life of the world.
We bless your holy Name, good Lord.

For men and women made in your image to rule in your Name over all that you have made:
We bless your holy Name, good Lord.

For the victory of light over darkness, and truth over error:
We bless your holy Name, good Lord.

For the knowledge of your prophetic word setting us free from fear and despair:
We bless your holy Name, good Lord.

For the advancement of your reign of justice and peace, of holiness and love:
We bless your holy Name, good Lord.

For the revelation of your Kingdom in our midst by your Son, Jesus Christ, who came on earth to manifest and to accomplish your will:
We bless your holy Name, good Lord.

For his humble birth and his holy life, and for his words and miracles:
We bless your holy Name, good Lord.

For his sufferings and death, and his entry into kingship by his resurrection and ascension:
We bless your holy Name, good Lord.

For the founding of the universal Church spread to the ends of the earth:
We bless your holy Name, good Lord.

For the coming of your Kingdom within us by the gifts of your Holy Spirit:
We bless your holy Name, good Lord.

For the advent of your Kingdom at the end of time when you will be all in all:
We bless your holy Name, good Lord.

PRAISE GOD: COMMON PRAYER AT TAIZÉ

•51 All the Blessings of This Life

Let us give thanks to the Lord:
For God's mercy and love are everlasting.

Father, through Jesus Christ and in the power of your Holy Spirit, receive
  our thanksgiving:
For the creation of the universe through your Word,
For making every human being in your image and likeness,
For the revelation of your purposes through the law and the prophets:
We give you thanks and praise.

For the gift of your Son, Jesus Christ our Lord,
For his lowly birth of Mary and for his baptism in the Jordan,
For his ministry of preaching, teaching and healing:
We give you thanks and praise.

For his steadfast love in going to Jerusalem,
For his agony in the garden of Gethsemane,
For his suffering and death on the Cross:
We give you thanks and praise.

For his resurrection from the dead and his ascension to your right hand in
  glory,
For his eternal intercession for us,
For his promise of his coming again to be our judge:
We give you thanks and praise.

For the outpouring of your Spirit on the Church,
For the commissioning of your Church to make disciples,
For the spreading of your kingdom throughout the world:
We give you thanks and praise.

Here special thanksgivings may be offered, and after each is said:
We give you thanks and praise.

So, Father, we give you grateful thanks for all your blessings.
We offer you our souls and bodies
To be a living sacrifice.
Send us out in the power of your Spirit
To live and work to your praise and glory. Amen.

THE METHODIST SERVICE BOOK*

•52 Grace Before Meals

Down through the centuries, God, you have provided for your people and
your creatures. Great is your faithfulness, O God!

As you gave the plants of the fields and the fruits of the trees to our first
parents:

So you give us food to eat, O Lord.

As you provided for Noah and his family in the ark:
So you give us food to eat, O Lord.

As you sent quail and manna to the Israelites while they traveled in the desert wilderness:
So you give us food to eat, O Lord.

As you declared that the oxen who thresh the grain should be given grain to eat:
So you give us food to eat, O Lord.

As you fed the hungry multitude and provided for your disciples:
So you give us food to eat, O Lord.

Great is your faithfulness, O God.
Great is your faithfulness, O God. Amen.

SAMUEL H. MILLER
–PRAYERS FOR DAILY USE

•53 Grace After Meals

God, our heavenly Father, created our world. God sustains it and nourishes it and cares for all his children. Let us praise God's name.

O Lord, the rain falls, earth thaws:
Holy and blessed is your name!

The sun shines, crops sprout and grow:
Holy and blessed is your name!

Farmers toil, grocers stock the food that graces our table:
Holy and blessed is your name!

Parents work, children help:
Holy and blessed is your name!

Rest and relaxation await us at the end of the day:
Holy and blessed is your name!

Food and drink are shared as signs of your abiding love:
Holy and blessed is your name!

Families and friends are made one in the breaking of bread:
Holy and blessed is your name!

Holy and blessed for ever. Amen.

TABLE PRAYERS

Prayer and Time

Advent to Pentecost

• 54 The Advent Antiphons

O Wisdom, Breath of the Most High, pervading and permeating all creation:
Come and make us friends of God.

O Lord of lords and Leader of the house of Israel, who appeared to Moses
in the burning bush and gave him your law on Sinai:
Come and save us with outstretched arm.

O Root of Jesse, standing as a signal to the nations, before whom all kings
are mute, to whom the nations will do homage:
Come and save us, delay no longer.

O Key of David and Ruler of the house of Israel, when you open nobody
can close, when you close nobody can open:
Come and proclaim liberty to captives and set the down-trodden free.

O radiant Dawn, Splendor of eternal light and Sun of justice:
Come and give light to those who live in darkness and the shadow of death.

O King of the nations, the Ruler they long for, the Cornerstone binding all
together:
Come and save the people you fashioned from the dust of the earth.

O Emmanuel, our King and our Lawgiver, the Anointed of the nations and
their Savior:
Come and save us, O Lord our God.

The spirit and the Bride say, Come!
Amen! Lord Jesus, come soon!

PRAY LIKE THIS*

•55 Veni Emmanuel

Two voices may lead this.

1: O come, O come, Emmanuel,
And ransom captive Israel,
That mourns in lonely exile here
Until the Son of God appear.
Rejoice! Rejoice!
Emmanuel shall come to thee, O Israel!

1: O come, thou Wisdom from on high,
Who ord'rest all things mightily;

2: To us the path of knowledge show,
And teach us in her ways to go.
Rejoice! Rejoice!
Emmanuel shall come to thee, O Israel!

2: O come, O come, thou Lord of might,
Who to thy tribes on Sinai's height,
In ancient times didst give the law,
In cloud, and majesty, and awe.
Rejoice! Rejoice!
Emmanuel shall come to thee, O Israel!

1: O come, thou Rod of Jesse's stem,
From every foe deliver them
That trust thy mighty power to save,
And give them vict'ry o'er the grave.
Rejoice! Rejoice!
Emmanuel shall come to thee, O Israel!

1: O come, thou Key of David, come,
And open wide our heav'nly home;

2: Make safe the way that leads on high,
And close the path to misery.
Rejoice! Rejoice!
Emmanuel shall come to thee, O Israel!

1: O come, thou Day-spring from on high,
And cheer us by thy drawing nigh;

2: Disperse the gloomy clouds of night,
And death's dark shadow put to flight.
Rejoice! Rejoice!
Emmanuel shall come to thee, O Israel!

2: O come, Desire of nations, bind
In one the hearts of humankind;
Bid thou our sad divisions cease,
And be thyself our King of Peace.
Rejoice! Rejoice!
Emmanuel shall come to thee, O Israel!
Amen.

LATIN CA. 9TH CENTURY*

• 56 Litany of the Incarnation

O God, the ruler of ages eternal,
you are without beginning or end:
Yet you choose to be born an infant in time.
  Praise to you, O Lord.

O God, the invisible,
you are the One whom nobody has seen or can see:
Yet you assume the face of the Son of Mary.
  Praise to you, O Lord.

O God, the all-powerful,
you hold the mountains in the palm of your hand:
Yet you let yourself be wrapped in swaddling clothes.
  Praise to you, O Lord.

O God, the eternal glory,
innumerable angels acclaim you endlessly:
Yet you choose to be rocked to sleep by the songs of the daughter of David.
  Praise to you, O Lord.

O God, the universal provider,
you feed every creature:
Yet you choose to hunger for the milk of your mother.
  Praise to you, O Lord.

O God, the infinite,
heaven and earth cannot contain you:
Yet you rest in the arms of Mary.
  Praise to you, O Lord.

O God, the perfect joy,
you are the source of the happiness of heaven and earth:
Yet you cry like a little child.

Praise to you, O Lord.

O God, the eternal Word,
you are the light of all created intelligence:
Yet you are laid in a manger and cannot even speak.
Praise to you, O Lord. Amen.

LUCIEN DEISS

From *Come, Lord Jesus,* © 1976, 1981 by Lucien Deiss.
Reprinted with permission.

•57 Glad Tidings of Great Joy

Blessed are you, Sun of righteousness, shining forth from the Father and
enlightening the whole universe.
Let heaven and earth rejoice!

Blessed are you, Lord Jesus Christ, reigning with the Father above the
cherubim, and worshiped by the seraphim.
Let heaven and earth rejoice!

Blessed are you, born as a little child and laid in a manger.
Let heaven and earth rejoice!

Blessed are you, humble offspring of a virgin, yet one with the Father.
Let heaven and earth rejoice!

Blessed are you, King of glory, graciously coming to dwell among us.
Let heaven and earth rejoice!

Blessed are you, giving us all we possess, yet accepting the gifts of the Wise
Men.
Let heaven and earth rejoice!

Blessed are you, our Bread of life, giving eternal life to our souls.
Let heaven and earth rejoice!

With the angelic host and all the heavenly powers, let us proclaim and
celebrate our Savior's birth.
Let heaven and earth rejoice!

With the spirits of the just made perfect, let us magnify and bless the Lord
to all eternity.
Let heaven and earth rejoice! Amen.

THE TAIZÉ OFFICE

•58 Christmas Present

Two voices may lead this.

1: For all who give you a face, Lord Jesus,
2: by spreading your love in the world:
We praise you.

1: For all who give you hands, Lord Jesus,
2: by doing their best toward their brothers and sisters:
We praise you.

1: For all who give you a mouth, Lord Jesus,
2: by defending the weak and the oppressed:
We praise you.

1: For all who give you eyes, Lord Jesus,
2: by seeing every bit of love in the heart of man and woman:
We praise you.

1: For all who give you a heart, Lord Jesus,
2: by preferring the poor to the rich, the weak to the strong:
We praise you.

1: For all who give to your poverty, Lord Jesus,
2: the look of hope for the Kingdom:
We praise you.

1: For all who reveal you simply by what they are, Lord Jesus,
2: because they reflect your beauty in their lives:
We praise you.

1: God our Father, you are the God of a thousand faces,
2: yet nothing can reveal you completely except the face of the child of Bethlehem:
We pray to you:
Continue in our lives the mystery of Christmas.
Let your Son become flesh in us
so that we may be for all our brothers and sisters
the revelation of your ever-present love. Amen.

LUCIEN DEISS

From *Come, Lord Jesus,* © 1976, 1981 by Lucien Deiss.
Reprinted with permission.

•59 Litany of the Magi

As the Wise Men of old followed the star:
Help us, O God, to follow the leading of your Spirit.

As they were led to the Savior:
Lead us, O God, to him who is the Way, the Truth and the Life.

As they brought treasures to the King:
Empower us, O God, to bring his gifts of faith and hope and love to the world.

As they fell down and worshiped the Child:
Inspire us, O God, to serve him every moment of our lives.

As Herod was kept from doing him harm:
Keep us, O God, from doing violence to his Name by thought or word or deed.

As Mary kept all things and pondered them in her heart:
Enable us, O God, to remember and to love.

As your Son shines forever as the Light of the world:
Shine forth in us, O God, that we may be lights of the world in our generation.

Holy Jesus, come from God:
Fill us now and always with your light. Amen.

ELMER N. WITT
–HELP IT ALL MAKE SENSE, LORD

•60 Epiphany

Almighty God, you did not forsake the world when it abandoned you; from ancient times you have made the promise of your victory shine before your people:
The joy of our hearts is in God!

Abraham hoped for your Christ and he also rejoiced to see his day, foretold by the prophets and desired by all the nations:
The joy of our hearts is in God!

The heavenly host celebrated his birth; apostles and martyrs, and the faithful throughout the ages have repeated the angels' song:
The joy of our hearts is in God!

Now, with your whole Church, we praise you; for our eyes have seen your salvation:
The joy of our hearts is in God!

Son of God, you became poor to make many rich; you humbled yourself and took the form of a slave, lifting us up to share in your glory:
The joy of our hearts is in God!

We were in darkness and you have given us light; we were without hope and we have received from your fullness grace upon grace:
The joy of our hearts is in God!

Dispose of us as you will; make us a people who will serve you in holiness; give us honest hearts to hear your word and bring forth in us abundant fruit to your honor and glory:
The joy of our hearts is in God!

Blessed be the Name of the Lord, Alleluia!
Henceforth and for evermore, Alleluia!

PRAISE GOD: COMMON PRAYER AT TAIZÉ

•61 The Baptism of Our Lord

O Christ, by your epiphany, light has shown on us to assure us of the fullness of salvation: grant your light to all whom we shall encounter today:
Kyrie eleison. (Lord, have mercy.)

O Christ, you humbled yourself and received baptism at your servant's hands, showing us the way of humility: grant us to serve humbly all the days of our life:
Kyrie eleison.

O Christ, by your baptism you washed away every impurity, making us children of the Father: grant the grace of adoption as God's children to all who are searching for him:
Kyrie eleison.

O Christ, by your baptism you sanctified the creation and opened the way of repentance and new life to all who are baptized: make us instruments of your Gospel in the world:
Kyrie eleison.

O Christ, by your baptism you revealed the Trinity, your Father calling you his beloved Son, through the Spirit descending upon you: renew a spirit of true worship in the royal priesthood of all the baptized.
Kyrie eleison.

O Christ, made manifest as the true light of God:
gladden our hearts on the joyful morning of your glory,

call us by our name on the great Day of your coming,
and give us grace to offer unending praise with all the hosts of heaven to
the Father in whom all things find their ending,
now and ever. Amen.

PRAISE GOD: COMMON PRAYER AT TAIZÉ

•62 Litany for an Ash Wednesday Eucharist

Following the Distribution of Ashes this may be said by the Presiding Minister and four
other voices.

The Lord our God has spoken to us:
"Turn to me now with all your heart,
with fasting, with weeping, and with mourning;
rend your hearts, not your garments."
We turn to you now, Father, and ask forgiveness.

1: Father, we have gazed on life and beauty, and on all that you have made,
    But we have refused to see you working among us, and refused to give
    you praise for all that you have given us.
    We turn to you now, Father, and ask forgiveness.

2: You call us to greatness, and we choose mediocrity;
    You place your trust in us, and we mistrust each other, ourselves, and
    you.
    We turn to you now, Father, and ask forgiveness.

3: You bid us spread peace, and our actions divide;
    You call us to build up, and our efforts tear down.
    We turn to you now, Father, and ask forgiveness.

4: You bid us spread your message of life, and we stockpile weapons of
    destruction;
    You give us cause to hope in humanity, and we blind our eyes with
    despair.
    We turn to you now, Father, and ask forgiveness.

The Presiding Minister says:

Father of mercy, and Father of love,
Look on us with kindness now
As we turn our gaze to you.
We have taken upon us this sign of repentance,
Proclaiming as we do that we are nothing
If we are not yours.
Ashes we were, and ashes we will be;
But you, our God, are God for ever and ever. Amen.

Following the Breaking of the Bread the Presiding Minister says:

This bread which we break is the new manna in the desert.
Though death stalk us like a lion or despair like a wolf, still this bread
of life will be ours to bless, break, and share.
Let us now pray to the Father:
Give us this day our daily bread.
Give us this day our daily bread.

When we are led into the desert, and our spirits wither like grass:
Give us this day our daily bread.

1:   When the fire of love dies down in us, and ashes threaten to choke our
souls:
Give us this day our daily bread.

2:   When we forget your promise, Lord, and our hope vanishes like smoke:
Give us this day our daily bread.

3:   When we are tempted to turn our faces and look away from our sisters
and brothers in need:
Give us this day our daily bread.

4:   When we taste the ashes of sorrow and forget the bread of life:
Give us this day our daily bread.

1-4: When we drift from this table of fellowship, and starve in the desert of
selfishness:
Give us this day our daily bread.

The Presiding Minister says:

Take now, and receive this meal
Given to us by Jesus for the forgiveness of sins.
Happy are those who are called to this supper.
Lord, I am not worthy to receive you,
but only say the word and I shall be healed.

The Distribution of the Communion now follows.

STEPHEN R. KOUDER, S.J.
–MODERN LITURGY

•63 The Acceptable Fast

"The fast that I like," says the Lord,
"is the breaking of the chains of evil,
the untying of the bonds of slavery."
Help us to fast, O Lord,
by loving our brothers and sisters.

"It is freeing the oppressed,
and welcoming the poor into your home."
Help us to fast, O Lord,
by loving our brothers and sisters.

"It is clothing the person you find naked,
and not despising your neighbor."
Help us to fast, O Lord,
by loving our brothers and sisters.

"Then will your light shine like the dawn,
and your wound be quickly healed over."
Help us to fast, O Lord,
by loving our brothers and sisters.

"Then, if you cry, God will answer;
if you call, God will say: I am here."
Help us to fast, O Lord,
by loving our brothers and sisters. Amen.

LUCIEN DEISS

From *Come, Lord Jesus,* © 1976, 1981 by Lucien Deiss. Reprinted with permission.

•64 In the Face of Temptation

O God, our Father, help us to resist the temptations which continually attack us.

Help us to resist the temptations which come from within and from our own natures:

The temptation to laziness and to too much love of ease and comfort;
The temptation to pride and self-conceit and to think of ourselves more
highly than we ought;
The temptation to put things off until it is too late ever to do them, and to
refuse to face the unpleasant things, until it is too late to do anything
about them:
Help us to resist these, O God.

The temptation to despair, and to lose heart and hope;
The temptation to lower our standards and to accept things as they are;
The temptation to be resignedly content with life as it is and ourselves as
we are:
Help us to resist these, O God.

The temptation to let passion and desire have their way;
The temptation to trade eternal happiness for the fleeting thrill of some
seductive moment;
The temptation to moodiness, to irritability, to bad temper;
The temptation to criticism, to fault-finding, to thinking the worst of
others:
Help us to resist these, O God.

Help us to resist the temptations which come to us from outside.

Help us to say No to every voice which invites us to leave your way.
Help us to resist every seduction which makes sin more attractive.
Help us to walk through the world, and yet to keep our garments
unspotted from the world.

*Help us to be wise enough never to play with fire; never to flirt with temptation;
never recklessly to put ourselves into a situation in which it is easy to go wrong;
never unthinkingly to develop habits which provide an opportunity for sin.*

Grant unto us that grace which will give us the strength and the purity ever
to overcome evil and to do the right; through Jesus Christ our Lord. *Amen.*

WILLIAM BARCLAY
–PRAYERS FOR THE CHRISTIAN YEAR

•65 . . . Tempted by the Devil

Let us pray, asking for the grace to follow Christ in sufferings, humiliations,
and death so as to enter with him into glory.

Silence

From the father of lies comes the promise that we shall be like gods.
And the truth is not in him.

From the father of lies comes the hope that we can be of more worth than
we already are.
And the truth is not in him.

From the father of lies comes the desire to possess more than we need.
And the truth is not in him.

From the father of lies comes the goal of a life of fame and honor.
And the truth is not in him.

From the desire of being esteemed, loved and sought after:
Jesus, deliver us.

From the desire of being praised, honored, and preferred:
Jesus, deliver us.

From the desire of being consulted, approved, and noticed:
Jesus, deliver us.

From the fear of being humbled, reproved, and slandered:
Jesus, deliver us.

From the fear of being forgotten, ridiculed, and reviled:
Jesus, deliver us.

Let us pray, asking our Lord to strengthen us with his power and to protect us from the deceptions of the father of lies.

Silence

Let us pray together to Christ our Savior.
Soul of Christ, sanctify me.
Body of Christ, save me.
Blood of Christ, inspire me.
Water from the side of Christ, wash me.
Passion of Christ, strengthen me.
O Good Jesus, hear me.
Hide me within your wounds.
Let me never be separated from you.

Defend me from the wicked enemy.
At the hour of my death call me, and bid me come into your presence,
That with your saints I may praise you for ever and ever. Amen.

SCRIPTURE SERVICES*

•66 Litany of Penitence

Most holy and merciful Father:
We confess to you and to one another,
and to the whole communion of saints
in heaven and on earth,
that we have sinned by our own fault
in thought, word, and deed;
by what we have done, and by what we have left undone.

We have not loved you with our whole heart, and mind, and strength. We have not loved our neighbors as ourselves. We have not forgiven others, as we have been forgiven.
Have mercy on us, Lord.

We have been deaf to your call to serve, as Christ served us. We have not been true to the mind of Christ. We have grieved your Holy Spirit.
Have mercy on us, Lord.

We confess to you, Lord, all our past unfaithfulness: the pride, hypocrisy, and impatience of our lives.
We confess to you, Lord.

Our self-indulgent appetites and ways, and our exploitation of other people:
We confess to you, Lord.

Our anger at our own frustration, and our envy of those more fortunate than ourselves:
We confess to you, Lord.

Our intemperate love of worldly goods and comforts, and our dishonesty in daily life and work:
We confess to you, Lord.

Our negligence in prayer and worship, and our failure to commend the faith that is in us:
We confess to you, Lord.

Accept our repentance, Lord, for the wrongs we have done: for our blindness to human need and suffering, and our indifference to injustice and cruelty:
Accept our repentance, Lord.

For all false judgments, for uncharitable thoughts toward our neighbors, and for our prejudice and contempt toward those who differ from us:
Accept our repentance, Lord.

For our waste and pollution of your creation, and our lack of concern for those who come after us:
Accept our repentance, Lord.

Restore us, good Lord, and let your anger depart from us:
Favorably hear us, for your mercy is great.

Accomplish in us the work of your salvation:
That we may show forth your glory in the world.

By the Cross and Passion of your Son our Lord:
Bring us with all your saints to the joy of his resurrection.

The Presiding Minister, facing the people, says:

Almighty God, the Father of our Lord Jesus Christ, who desires not the death of sinners, but rather that they may turn from their wickedness and live, has given power and commandment to his ministers to declare and pronounce to his people, being penitent, the absolution and remission of their sins. God pardons and absolves all those who truly repent, and with sincere hearts believe his holy Gospel.

Therefore we beseech God to grant us true repentance and his Holy Spirit, that those things may please God which we do on this day, and that the rest of our life hereafter may be pure and holy, so that at the last we may come to his eternal joy; through Jesus Christ our Lord. *Amen.*

THE BOOK OF COMMON PRAYER 1979

•67 Palm Sunday

Who is this riding among us?
Jesus, the Prophet of Nazareth.

Blessed is he who comes in the Name of God.
Hosanna, may his Way be victorious.

Who is this riding the animal of peace?
Jesus, the Prophet of Nazareth.

Blessed be the coming Kingdom of David.
Hosanna, may his Way be victorious.

Who is the Liberator of Israel?
Jesus, the Prophet of Nazareth.

Blessed be the freedom he brings.
Hosanna, may his Way be victorious.

Who is this carrying the palm of peace?
Jesus, the Prophet of Nazareth.

Blessed be our leader, the Prince of peace.
Hosanna, may his Way be victorious.

Who is this that destroys the weapons of war?
Jesus, the Prophet of Nazareth.

Blessed is he who comes in the Name of God.
Hosanna, may his Way be victorious.

Who is this that frees the oppressed from prison?
Jesus, the Prophet of Nazareth.

Blessed is he who releases all captives.
Hosanna, may his Way be victorious.

Who is this that makes wars to cease in all the world?
Jesus, the Prophet of Nazareth.

Blessed is he who restores the Paradise of Eden.
Hosanna, may his Way be victorious.

THE COVENANT OF PEACE
–A LIBERATION PRAYER BOOK*

• 68 Dayyenu: It Would Have Been Enough

The original Hebrew response used at the Passover Seder may be said after each reason for celebration and thanksgiving, or otherwise the English equivalent.

If God had created us and not revealed himself in all his marvelous works:
Dayyenu. (It would have been enough.)

If God had revealed himself and not made a covenant with his people:
Dayyenu.

If God had made a covenant with his people and not breathed his Spirit into us:
Dayyenu.

If God had breathed his Spirit into us and not shared with us his love:
Dayyenu.

If God had shared his love with us and not watched over us when we strayed from him:
Dayyenu.

104

If God had watched over us when we strayed from him and not delivered us from the bonds of slavery:
Dayyenu.

If God had delivered us from the bonds of slavery and not led us into a land of freedom:
Dayyenu.

If God had led us into a land of freedom and not sent us holy men and women to speak to us of his love:
Dayyenu.

If God had sent us holy men and women to speak to us of his love and not promised us a Savior:
Dayyenu.

If God had promised us a Savior and not sent us his own beloved Son:
Dayyenu.

If God had had sent us Jesus, his own beloved Son, and had he not become our very brother:
Dayyenu.

If Jesus had become our very brother and not shared our joy and sorrows, our laughter and tears:
Dayyenu.

If Jesus had shared our life and not taught us how to forgive each other:
Dayyenu.

If Jesus had taught us how to forgive each other and had not shown us how to love:
Dayyenu.

If Jesus had taught us how to love and had not taught us how to serve each other:
Dayyenu.

If Jesus had shown us how to serve each other and had not left us this supper *(eucharist)* as a reminder of his love:
Dayyenu.

If Jesus had left us this supper *(eucharist)* as a reminder of his love and not called us to carry on his work in the world:
Dayyenu.

But as it is, Father, your Son Jesus has revealed your love for us. His whole life, his death and his resurrection from the dead testify to your deep mercy and compassion. Therefore, Father, we bless and thank you, we praise and worship you with all creation, for you are worthy of our worship, and beyond all the praises of our hearts. To you and to your Son, Jesus, and to the Holy Spirit belong all glory, now and for ever. *Amen.*

MICHAEL E. MOYNAHAN, S.J.
–MODERN LITURGY*

• 69 The Solemn Prayers of Good Friday

These prayers may be used either in part or in their entirety.

1. For the Church:

Let us pray, dear friends,
for the holy Church of God throughout the world,
that God the almighty Father
may guide it and gather it together
so that we may worship God
in peace and tranquility.

Silence

Almighty and eternal God,
you have shown your glory to all nations
in Christ, your Son.
Guide the work of your Church.
Help it to persevere in faith,
proclaim your name,
and bring your salvation to people everywhere.

We ask this through Christ our Lord. Amen.

2. For the Pope:

Let us pray
for our Holy Father, Pope _____,
that God who chose him to be bishop
may give him health and strength
to guide and govern God's holy people.

Silence

Almighty and eternal God,
you guide all things by your word,
you govern all Christian people.
In your love protect the Pope you have chosen for us.
Under his leadership deepen our faith

and make us better Christians.

We ask this through Christ our Lord. Amen.

3. For the People of God:

Let us pray
for _____, our bishop,
for all bishops, priests, and deacons;
for all who have a special ministry in the Church,
and for all God's people.

Silence

Almighty and eternal God,
your Spirit guides the Church
and makes it holy.
Listen to our prayers
and help each of us
in our own vocation
to do your work more faithfully.

We ask this through Christ our Lord. Amen.

4. For those preparing for Baptism:

Let us pray for those [*among us*] preparing for baptism,
that God in his mercy
may make them responsive to his love,
forgive their sins through the waters of new birth,
and give them life in Jesus Christ our Lord.

Silence

Almighty and eternal God,
you continually bless your Church with new members.
Increase the faith and understanding
of those [among us] preparing for baptism.
Give them a new birth in these living waters
and make them members of your chosen family.

We ask this through Christ our Lord. Amen.

5. For the unity of Christians:

Let us pray
for all our brothers and sisters
who share our faith in Jesus Christ,
that God may gather and keep together in one Church

all those who seek the truth with sincerity.

Silence

Almighty and eternal God,
you keep together those you have united.
Look kindly on all who follow Jesus your Son.
We are all consecrated to you by our common baptism.
Make us one in the fullness of faith,
and keep us one in the fellowship of love.

We ask this through Christ our Lord. Amen.

6. For the Jewish People:

Let us pray
for the Jewish people,
the first to hear the word of God,
that they may continue to grow in the love of his Name
and in faithfulness to his covenant.

Silence

Almighty and eternal God,
long ago you gave your promise to Abraham and his posterity.
Listen to your Church as we pray
that the people you first made your own
may arrive at the fullness of redemption.

We ask this through Christ our Lord. Amen.

7. For those who do not believe in Christ:

Let us pray
for those who do not believe in Christ,
that the light of the Holy Spirit
may show them the way to salvation.

Silence

Almighty and eternal God,
enable those who do not acknowledge Christ
to find the truth
as they walk before you in sincerity of heart.
Help us to grow in love for one another,
to grasp more fully the mystery of your godhead,
and to become more perfect witnesses of your love
in the sight of all.

We ask this through Christ our Lord. Amen.

8. For those who do not believe in God:

Let us pray
for those who do not believe in God,
that they may find God
by sincerely following all that is right.

Silence

Almighty and eternal God,
you created the human race
so that all might long to find you
and have peace when you are found.
Grant that, in spite of the hurtful things
that stand in their way,
they may all recognize in the lives of Christians
the tokens of your love and mercy,
and gladly acknowledge you
as the one true God and Father of us all.

We ask this through Christ our Lord. Amen.

9. For all in public office:

Let us pray for those who serve us in public office,
that God may guide their minds and hearts,
so that all people everywhere may live in true peace and freedom.

Silence

Almighty and eternal God,
you know the longings of human hearts
and you protect our human rights.
In your goodness
watch over those in authority,
so that people everywhere may enjoy
religious freedom, security, and peace.

We ask this through Christ our Lord. Amen.

10. For all in special need:

Let us pray, dear friends,
that God the almighty Father
may heal the sick,
comfort the dying,

give safety to travelers,
free those unjustly deprived of liberty,
and rid the world of falsehood,
hunger, and disease.

Silence

Almighty, ever-living God,
you give strength to the weary
and new courage to those who have lost heart.
Hear the prayers of all who call on you in any trouble
that they may have the joy of receiving your help in their need.

We ask this through Christ our Lord. Amen.

THE ENGLISH TRANSLATION OF THE ROMAN MISSAL, 1973*

•70 . . . They Crucified Him

O God, the lover of humankind,
we remember before you
all who took part in Christ's passion
from evil or from good:

The priests and Pharisees and elders
    who conspired to arrest him;
Judas, his disciple,
    who betrayed him with a kiss;
the apostles who deserted him,
    yet bore witness to his glory on the Cross:
Have mercy on them and us.

Malchus, struck by Peter's sword,
    whom Jesus touched and healed;
the young man who followed Jesus,
    yet fled naked from the crowd;
the high priest's maids and servants
    before whom Peter denied the Lord:
Have mercy on them and us.

Annas, the high priest's father-in-law,
    who handed Jesus to Caiaphas;
Caiaphas, the high priest,
    who convicted him of blasphemy;

the chief priests, scribes, and officers
   who mocked and beat him
   and condemned him as worthy of death:
Have mercy on them and us.

Herod the king
   who arrayed him in gorgeous apparel
   and treated him with contempt;
The Roman soldiers
   who clothed him in purple
   and put a crown of thorns on his head
   and pretended to worship him;
the people who once had welcomed him
   but now taunted him and required his death:
Have mercy on them and us.

Pilate's wife who begged her husband
   to be innocent of the blood of this righteous man;
Barabbas, the robber and murderer,
   whose condemnation was exchanged for Christ's;
Pontius Pilate, who delivered Jesus to be crucified,
   yet confessed him the Man and our King:
Have mercy on them and us.

Simon of Cyrene, a passer-by,
   who was compelled to follow Jesus
   and bear his Cross;
the women of Jerusalem,
   bewailing and lamenting him,
   whom Jesus told to weep for themselves and their children;
the soldiers who nailed him to the Cross
   and whom Jesus prayed his Father to forgive:
Have mercy on them and us.

The crowd that scoffed at him
   as one who saved others
   but could not save himself;
the thieves crucified with him,
   the one who reviled him,
   the other who asked to be remembered in his Kingdom;
the unknown man
   who heard his cry of desolation
   and ran to quench his thirst:
Have mercy on them and us.

Mary, his mother,
  who stood by the Cross of her dying son,
  and was made the mother of the disciple whom he loved;
the centurion
  who watched when he gave up the spirit
  and proclaimed him the Son of God;
the women who had followed him and ministered to him
  and stood either near or afar,
  among them
  Mary Magdalene, Mary the mother of James and Joseph, his mother's
  sister, Mary the wife of Cleopas, and Salome, the mother of James
  and John:
Have mercy on them and us.

Almighty and eternal God,
  by the Cross of your beloved Son
  joy has come into the world:
  grant that all who were with him when he suffered
  may share the victory he accomplished by his death.
Have mercy on them and us.

Silence

Eternal God,
  you have called people everywhere not to certainty
  but to trust in your faithfulness:
  give your grace to those who are tempted
  to deny the holy insecurity of faith,
  that they may take the risk of self-abandonment
  to him who abandoned himself on the Cross for us,
  even Jesus Christ our Lord. *Amen.*

Holy Father,
  whose only Son gave himself to us
  without limit and without reserve,
  and who fills us with the love
  by which to love others:
  enable us to give ourselves to our enemies and friends
  so that they may know the immeasurable love
  which is in Christ Jesus our Lord;
  who is alive and reigns with you and the Holy Spirit,
  one God, now and for ever. Amen.

RAYMOND HOCKLEY*

•71 The Passion of Our Lord

The response "Have mercy on us" is said throughout.

Jesus, Son of God and Redeemer of the world: *Have mercy on us.*
Jesus, sold by Judas for thirty pieces of silver:
Jesus, praying in Gethsemane:
Jesus, strengthened by an angel:
Jesus, betrayed by a friend with a kiss:
Jesus, bound by the soldiers and forsaken by the disciples:
Jesus, brought before Annas and Caiaphas:
Jesus, struck in the face by a servant:
Jesus, accused by false witnesses:
Jesus, found guilty and sentenced to death:
Jesus, spat upon, blindfolded and struck on the cheek:
Jesus, denied three times by Peter:
Jesus, delivered up to Pilate:
Jesus, despised and mocked by Herod:
Jesus, rejected in favor of Barabbas:
Jesus, torn with scourges and bruised for our sins:
Jesus, covered with a purple robe and crowned with thorns:
Jesus, demanded for crucifixion by your own people:
Jesus, condemned to an ignominious death:
Jesus, laden with the heavy weight of the Cross:
Jesus, led like a sheep to the slaughter:
Jesus, stripped of your garments and fastened with nails to the Cross:
Jesus, reviled by the criminals and promising paradise to the penitent thief:
Jesus, commending Saint John to your mother as her son:
Jesus, declaring yourself forsaken by your Father:
Jesus, in your thirst given gall and vinegar to drink:
Jesus, testifying that all things written concerning you have been
    accomplished:
Jesus, commending your spirit into the hands of the Father:
Jesus, pierced with a lance and taken down from the Cross:
Jesus, laid in the sepulchre:
Jesus, rising glorious from the dead:
Jesus, ascending into heaven and praying to the Father ever on our behalf:
Jesus, coming again to judge the living and the dead:

Lamb of God, you take away the sins of the world:
    have mercy on us.
Lamb of God, you take away the sins of the world:
    have mercy on us.

Lamb of God, you take away the sins of the world:
grant us peace. Amen.

KYRIE ELEISON

•72 The Cross of Christ

Lord, when we pity ourselves and think we make great sacrifices for others:
Remind us of your life-giving sacrifice on the Cross.

Lord, when our patience wears thin and we are ready to give up:
Speak to us through the example of your endurance on the Cross.

Lord, when we get angry and wish to retaliate against our enemies:
Bring to our remembrance your words to your enemies from the Cross.

Lord, when we feel rejected or persecuted for doing what is right and good:
Sustain us by the knowledge of how you were reviled and rejected on the Cross.

Lord, when we suffer pain of body or anguish of mind in this life:
Keep us near the Cross.

Lord, when we are afraid to stand for that which is true and honorable:
Strengthen us with the courage with which you went to the Cross.

Lord, when we feel alone in the world, forsaken and forgotten:
Comfort us with your love made known on the Cross.

Lord, when we come to the time of our own death:
Uphold us with the assurance that life did not end for you on the Cross.

Lord, when we are tempted by despair or fear of what lies ahead:
Fill us with the hope of resurrection and new life which are the fruits of your Cross. Amen.

LARRY HARD

•73 The Folly of the Cross

The message about Christ's death on the cross is nonsense to those who are being lost, but for us who are being saved, it is God's power . . . For God in his wisdom made it impossible for people to know him by means of their own wisdom. Instead, God decided to save those who believe by means of the "foolish" message we preach. Jews want miracles for proof, and Greeks

look for wisdom. As for us, we proclaim Christ on the Cross, a message that is offensive to the Jews and nonsense to the Gentiles; but for those whom God has called, both Jews and Gentiles, this message is Christ, who is the power of God and the wisdom of God.
(I Corinthians 1:18, 21–25)

Let us glory in the Cross of our Lord Jesus Christ,
for in him it is our salvation, life and resurrection.

Let us pray.

Silence

Like travelers lost in a parched and burning desert:
We cry to you, O Lord.

Like men shipwrecked on a lonely coast:
We cry to you, O Lord.

Like a mother robbed of a crust of bread that she was bringing to her starving children:
We cry to you, O Lord.

Like a prisoner unjustly confined to a dank and gloomy dungeon:
We cry to you, O Lord.

Like a slave torn by the master's lash:
We cry to you, O Lord.

Like an innocent person led to execution:
We cry to you, O Lord.

Like all the nations of the earth before the day of their deliverance dawned:
We cry to you, O Lord.

Like Christ on the Cross when he cried out: "My God, my God, why have you forsaken me?"
We cry to you, O Lord.

By your Cross, Lord Jesus Christ,
the Church is redeemed, sanctified and raised on high.
Protect us, O Lord who take refuge beneath the wings of your Cross
and wash us in the precious blood and the water of life,
flowing from your wounded side,
O Savior of the world,
for you live and reign for ever and ever. Amen.

PRAISE HIM!

•74 Psalm 22

Let us pray, meditating with the Psalmist on the sufferings of our Redeemer and asking the Lamb of God to wash us in the cleansing stream of his Blood.

Silence

My God, my God, why have you forsaken me,
far from my prayer, from the words of my cry?
Lamb of God, you take away the sins of the world,
have mercy on us.

O my God, I cry out by day, and you answer not;
by night, and there is no relief for me.
Lamb of God, you take away the sins of the world,
have mercy on us.

But I am a worm, and not a man;
the scorn of all and despised by the people.
Lamb of God, you take away the sins of the world,
have mercy on us.

All who see me scoff at me;
they mock me with parted lips, they wag their heads.
Lamb of God, you take away the sins of the world,
have mercy on us.

I am like water poured out;
all my bones are out of joint.
Lamb of God, you take away the sins of the world,
have mercy on us.

They have pierced my hands and my feet;
I can count all my bones.
Lamb of God, you take away the sins of the world,
have mercy on us.

They look on and gloat over me;
they divide my garments among them,
and for my clothing they cast lots.
Lamb of God, you take away the sins of the world,
have mercy on us.

"Worthy is the Lamb who was slain
to receive power and wealth
and wisdom and strength
and honor and glory and blessing."

Lord God, Lamb of God, Son of the Father,
you take away the sins of the world, have mercy on us. Amen.

SCRIPTURE SERVICES

• 75 The Reproaches

The following may be recited in the presence of the Cross or otherwise during
its veneration by the assembled congregation.

My people, what have I done unto you?
or in what have I offended you? Answer me.
Because you led us out of the land of bondage,
we have prepared a cross for our Savior.

Silence

Holy God, Holy God:
Holy, mighty One. Holy, mighty One.
Holy immortal One, have mercy on us.
Holy immortal One, have mercy on us.

Because you led us out through the desert forty years,
and fed us with manna, and brought us into a very good land,
we have prepared a cross for our Savior.

Silence

Holy God, Holy God:
Holy, mighty One. Holy, mighty One.
Holy immortal One, have mercy on us.
Holy immortal One, have mercy on us.

What more should I have done, and did it not?
Behold, I have planted you as my fairest vine:
And we have become very bitter to you,
for we have quenched your thirst with vinegar,
and with a lance we have pierced our Savior's side.

Silence

Holy God, Holy God:
Holy, mighty One. Holy, mighty One.
Holy immortal One, have mercy on us.
Holy immortal One, have mercy on us.

My people, what have I done unto you?

or in what have I offended you? Answer me.

Silence

Holy God, Holy God:
Holy, mighty One. Holy, mighty One.
Holy immortal One, have mercy on us.
Holy immortal One, have mercy on us. Amen.

–ADAPTED FROM TRADITIONAL MATERIAL*

• 76 The Mystery of the Cross

The Cross is a confusion for us.
There is mystery in the Cross.

The Cross is a paradox which we do not understand.
There is mystery in the Cross.

The Cross is an absurdity:
Yet it bears an inner truth.

We see in the Cross an instrument of death:
Yet we acknowledge in it the way of salvation.

We see in the Cross the abandonment of Jesus by the Father:
Yet we acknowledge the crucified Jesus as the way to the Father.

We see life poured out on the Cross:
Yet we acknowledge life gathered in the one person of Jesus.

We see death on the Cross:
Yet we acknowledge life through the Cross.

We see the scattering of disciples in the face of the Cross:
Yet we acknowledge the subsequent gathering of disciples around the
transformed Jesus.

We see the wood of the Cross as an instrument of defeat:
Yet we acknowledge the Cross as the symbol and banner of victory.

We see a sinless and innocent person put to death on the Cross:
Yet we acknowledge the ransom of a sinful people.

We see the bleakness of the Cross:
Yet we acknowledge the Cross as a royal throne.

We see the suffering of the Nazarene on the Cross:
Yet we acknowledge the redemptive self-giving of the Son of God.

We see the painful lifting up of Jesus on the Cross:
Yet we acknowledge the glorious exaltation of Christ above the earth.

We see the life of Jesus draining out of him on the Cross:
Yet we acknowledge his life filling a reconciled world.

We see the weakness of a dying man on the Cross:
Yet we acknowledge the power of a living Lord on the Cross.

We see Jesus handed over to executioners:
Yet we acknowledge his power to control the events of life and death.

We see a servant on the Cross:
Yet we acknowledge a Lord.

There is mystery in the Cross:
And absurd joy.

There is mystery in the Cross:
And life and peace and hope.

We adore you, O Christ, and we bless you:
Because by your holy Cross you have redeemed the world. Amen.

ABBOT JEROME THEISEN, O.S.B.*

•77 Lift High the Cross

Leader and People: (Refrain)

Lift high the Cross, the love of Christ proclaim
Till all the world adore his sacred name.

Come, Christians, follow where our Captain trod,
Our King victorious, Christ, the Son of God.
Refrain.

Led on their way by this triumphant sign,
The hosts of God in conqu'ring ranks combine.
Refrain.

Each new-born soldier of the Crucified
Bears on the brow the seal of him who died.
Refrain.

This is the sign which Satan's legions fear
And angels veil their faces to revere.
Refrain.

Saved by this Cross whereon their Lord was slain,
Earth's sons and daughters their lost home regain.
Refrain.

From north and south, from east and west they raise
In growing unison their song of praise.
Refrain.

O Lord, once lifted on the glorious Tree,
As thou hast promised, draw us all to thee.
Refrain.

Let every race and every language tell
Of him who saves our souls from death and hell.
Refrain.

From farthest regions let them homage bring,
And on his Cross adore their Savior King.
Refrain.

Set up thy throne, that earth's despair may cease
Beneath the shadow of its healing peace.
Refrain.

For thy blest Cross which doth for all atone
Creation's praises rise before thy throne.
Refrain.

So shall our song of triumph ever be:
Praise to the Crucified for victory.
Refrain. Amen.

GEORGE W. KITCHIN AND MICHAEL R. NEWBOLT*

•78 Confessions at the Empty Tomb

Lord, Jesus Christ,
we come to the lonely Cross:
And we see you stripped,
we see you murdered,
we see you deserted.

Lord, Jesus Christ,
we come to the empty tomb:

And we see our death,
  we see our own tomb,
  we see our own emptiness.

Lord, Jesus Christ,
when we come to the empty tomb:
We remember how we treated
  our parents,
  our friends,
  our neighbors,
  our Lord,
  and we feel sorry for ourselves.

Lord, Jesus Christ,
when we come to the empty tomb:
We see a hungry world before us,
  the pain of starving children,
  the guilt of war on our hands,
  the terror of fellow human beings without rights,
  and we know that we share in these evils.

Lord, Jesus Christ,
when we come to the empty tomb:
We search inside ourselves
  and we cannot escape what we are,
  people caught in our selfish love,
  our cold hypocrisy,
  our depressions,
  our loneliness,
  and our frustrations.

Lord, Jesus Christ,
when we come to the empty tomb:
We face you as never before,
  as the one forgotten,
  as the one oppressed,
  as the one pushed aside,
  as the one left out.

Lord, Jesus Christ,
we come to the empty tomb:
To confess our guilt,
  our pain,
  our emptiness,
  and to look for hope from you. Amen.

NORMAN C. HABEL

• 79 Litany of Hope

Let us pray that our hope will grow more and more strong within us.

Silence

"My child, when you come to serve the Lord, prepare yourself for trials."
Into your hands I commend my spirit:
You will redeem me, O Lord, my faithful God.

"Be sincere of heart and steadfast, undisturbed in time of adversity."
Into your hands I commend my spirit:
You will redeem me, O Lord, my faithful God.

"Accept whatever befalls you, in crushing misfortune be patient."
Into your hands I commend my spirit:
You will redeem me, O Lord, my faithful God.

"Trust God, and God will help you; make straight your ways and hope in
him."
Into your hands I commend my spirit:
You will redeem me, O Lord, my faithful God.

"You who fear the Lord, wait for God's mercy, turn not away lest you fall."
Into your hands I commend my spirit:
You will redeem me, O Lord, my faithful God.

"You who fear the Lord, hope for good things, for lasting joy and mercy."
Into your hands I commend my spirit:
You will redeem me, O Lord, my faithful God.

"Study the generations long past and understand; has anyone hoped in the
Lord and been disappointed?"
Into your hands I commend my spirit:
You will redeem me, O Lord, my faithful God.

O Lord our God, your faithfulness and kindness to us will never come to an
end. Grant us, we pray you, the gift of an unswerving trust and confidence
in the promises which you make to us. Fulfill our hopes through him who is
the Anchor of our hope, Jesus Christ our Lord. *Amen!*

SCRIPTURE SERVICES

•80 The Paschal Victory

Let us pray, thanking God for the victory that Jesus, God's Son and our Brother, has won by his death and resurrection. It is for us that he has triumphed.

Silence

Christ died for all, in order that they who are alive may live no longer for themselves, but for him who died for them and rose again.
Thanks be to God who has given us the victory through our Lord Jesus Christ.

If then any are in Christ, they are a new creation: the former things have passed away: behold, they are made new.
Thanks be to God who has given us the victory through our Lord Jesus Christ.

For God, who commanded light to shine out of darkness, has shone in our hearts, to give enlightenment concerning the knowledge of the glory of God, shining on the face of Christ Jesus.
Thanks be to God who has given us the victory through our Lord Jesus Christ.

For you were once darkness, but now you are light in the Lord.
Thanks be to God who has given us the victory through our Lord Jesus Christ.

Walk, then, as children of light, for the fruit of the light is in all goodness and justice and truth, and test what is well pleasing to God.
Thanks be to God who has given us the victory through our Lord Jesus Christ.

For if we live, we live to the Lord, or if we die, we die to the Lord.
Whether we live or die, we are the Lord's.

You were buried together with Christ in Baptism, and in him also you rose again through faith in the working of God who raised him from the dead.
Whether we live or die, we are the Lord's.

"Death is swallowed up in victory! O death, where is thy victory? O death, where is thy sting?"
Thanks be to God who has given us the victory through our Lord Jesus Christ. Amen.

SCRIPTURE SERVICES

•81 Easter Hymn

The shadows seized a body:
And found it was God.

They reached for earth:
And what they held was heaven.

They took what they could see:
It was what no one sees.

Where is death's goad?
Where is the shadow's victory?

Christ is risen:
The world below is in ruins.

Christ is risen:
The spirits of evil are fallen.

Christ is risen:
The angels of God are rejoicing.

Christ is risen:
The tombs are void of their dead.

Christ has indeed arisen from the dead:
The first of those who sleep.

Glory and power are his for ever and ever. Amen.

HIPPOLYTUS OF ROME, EARLY 3RD CENTURY*

• 82 The Risen Lord

Lord Jesus, by your resurrection,
you renew the universe;
you change our death into your life;
    we pray to you:
Jesus Christ, risen Lord, have mercy on us.

Give us kindness wherever you find bitterness,
confidence wherever you find distress,
joy wherever you find sorrow;
    we pray to you:
Jesus Christ, risen Lord, have mercy on us.

Give us humility wherever pride reigns,
pardon wherever offense abides,
grace wherever sin abounds;
    we pray to you:
Jesus Christ, risen Lord, have mercy on us.

Give us love wherever hatred burns,
hope wherever despair is crying,
faith wherever doubt prevails;
  we pray to you:
Jesus Christ, risen Lord, have mercy on us.

Give us a new spirit in our old age,
a new heart to replace a heart of stone,
and the New Covenant in your holy resurrection;
  we pray to you:
Jesus Christ, risen Lord, have mercy on us. Amen.

LUCIEN DEISS

From *Come, Lord Jesus,* © 1976, 1981 by Lucien Deiss.
Reprinted with permission.

•83 An Ascensiontide Litany

Leader and People:

See the Conqu'ror mounts in triumph; see the King in royal state,
Riding on the clouds, his chariot, to his heav'nly palace gate!
Hark! the choirs of angel voices joyful alleluias sing,
And the portals high are lifted to receive their heav'nly King.

O Christ, through your Ascension, you raised our human nature above all
principalities and powers, and gave it power over everything in heaven and on
earth:
King of glory, intercede for us.

O Christ, through your Ascension, you prepared for us mortal creatures a
dwelling place in heaven, that we might dwell there in everlasting life:
King of glory, intercede for us.

O Christ, through your Ascension, you led forth the captives you had
liberated and poured out your gifts upon all who believe in you:
King of glory, intercede for us.

Christ who on the cross did suffer, Christ who from the grave arose,
Christ has vanquished sin and Satan; Christ by death has spoiled his foes.
While he lifts his hands in blessing, Christ is parted from his friends;
While their eager eyes behold him, Christ upon the clouds ascends.

O Christ, you rose up to heaven in a cloud, and will return again in the
same manner with glory:
King of glory, intercede for us.

O Christ, you sit at the right hand of the Father who sent you:

King of glory, intercede for us.

O Christ, you exalted our humanity to heaven, and conferred upon us the royal priesthood:
King of glory, intercede for us.

You have raised our human nature on the clouds to God's right hand:
There we sit in heav'nly places, there with you in glory stand.
Jesus reigns, adored by angels; man with God is on the throne;
Mighty Lord, in your Ascension, we by faith behold our own. Amen.

THE TAIZÉ OFFICE
–HYMN STANZAS BY CHRISTOPHER WORDSWORTH*

• 84 The Lord Reigns!

Worthy is the Lamb who has been slain to receive power, and riches, and wisdom, and might, and honor, and glory, and blessing.
Unto the Lamb be glory!

Unto him who sits on the throne, and unto the Lamb, be blessing, and honor, and glory, and dominion, for ever and ever.
Unto the Lamb be glory!

Worthy are you, for you were slain, and did purchase unto God with your blood people of every tribe, and tongue, and race, and nation.
Unto the Lamb be glory!

Salvation unto our God who sits on the throne, and unto the Lamb.
Blessing and glory, and wisdom, and thanksgiving, and honor, and power, and might, be unto our God for ever and ever. Amen.

THE CHURCH OF SOUTH INDIA*

• 85 A Litany for Pentecost

When the day of Pentecost had come they were all together in one place and all of the many foreigners heard the witnesses speaking in their own tongue.
Come, Holy Spirit, witness to us also in our several languages.

Speak in the language of our need.
Let us hear how our deepest hungers, desires, and aspirations can be fulfilled by your goodness and in your service.
Come, Holy Spirit, give us that good news again.

Speak in the language of our fear.
Let us hear how our worries about the future, and about each other, and about ourselves, can find rest in your providential care.
Come, Holy Spirit, give us that encouraging news again.

Speak in the language of our guilt.
Let us hear how our confessed shame for wrong things done and for good things undone is covered by your forgiveness.
Come, Holy Spirit, give us that liberating news again.

Speak in the language of our gratitude.
Let us hear how our honest thanks relate us, not only to those with whom we live, but also to you, the Lord and Giver of life.
Come, Holy Spirit, give us that enlarging news again.

Speak to us in the language of joy.
Let us hear how our gladness and our delight not only brighten this world, but honor you who made the world.
Come, Holy Spirit, give us that enlivening word again.

Speak to us in the language of hope.
Let us hear how our yearning and our expectations are not just wishful thinking, but responses to your promise.
Come, Holy Spirit, give us that good news again.

For all your Spirit's illuminations,
and all your Spirit's quickening powers,
we praise you, Father, on this Pentecost,
in the name of your Son. Amen.

MODELS FOR MINISTERS I*

• 86 Litany of the Holy Spirit

O Holy Spirit, who at the beginning moved upon the face of the waters:
Have mercy upon us.

O Holy Spirit, by whose inspiration holy men and women spoke of old as they were moved:
Have mercy upon us.

O Holy Spirit, power of the highest, who overshadowed Mary:
Have mercy upon us.

O Holy Spirit, through whom the holy Child Jesus grew strong in faith, and was filled with wisdom:

Have mercy upon us.

O Holy Spirit, who descended like a dove, and alighted upon Christ our Lord at his baptism:
Have mercy upon us.

O Holy Spirit, by whom Jesus was led up into the wilderness to be tempted of the devil:
Have mercy upon us.

O Holy Spirit, through whom Christ offered himself without spot to God:
Have mercy upon us.

O Holy Spirit, who on the Day of Pentecost descended upon the apostles in the likeness of fiery tongues:
Have mercy upon us.

O Holy Spirit, by whom we have been brought out of darkness and error into the clear light and true knowledge of God, and of his Son Jesus Christ:
Have mercy upon us.

O Holy Spirit, by whom the whole body of the Church is governed and sanctified:
Have mercy upon us.

O Holy Spirit, by whom we were born to new life in Baptism:
Have mercy upon us.

O Holy Spirit, interceding for us with groanings that cannot be uttered:
Have mercy upon us.

O Holy Spirit, by whom the love of God is shed abroad in our hearts:
Have mercy upon us.

By your life-giving power and might:
Deliver us, O Holy Spirit.

By your all-powerful intercession:
Deliver us, O Holy Spirit.

By your continual abiding in the Church:
Deliver us, O Holy Spirit.

We beseech you to hear us, O Holy Spirit, that it may please you to guide your holy Church universal into all truth, and to fill it with your love:
Hear us, O Holy Spirit.

That we may strive to keep the unity of the Spirit in the bond of peace:
Hear us, O Holy Spirit.

That, as we live in the Spirit, we may also walk in the Spirit:

Hear us, O Holy Spirit.

That we may grow in grace, and in the knowledge of our Lord and Savior Jesus Christ:
Hear us, O Holy Spirit.

That with sincerity of purpose we may seek in all things God's greater glory:
Hear us, O Holy Spirit.

That, in all our thoughts, words, and works, we may be conformed more and more to the life and passion of the Lord Jesus:
Hear us, O Holy Spirit.

That we may be filled with your sevenfold gift: the spirit of wisdom and understanding, the spirit of counsel and ghostly strength, the spirit of knowledge and true godliness, and the spirit of your most holy fear:
Hear us, O Holy Spirit.

That we may ever be mindful of that solemn account, which, for ourselves and others, we must one day give at the judgment-seat of Christ:
Hear us, O Holy Spirit.

That we may have grace to persevere unto the end:
Hear us, O Holy Spirit.

Holy Spirit:
We beseech you to hear us.

Lord and Giver of life:
We beseech you to hear us.

Lord, have mercy upon us.
Christ, have mercy upon us.
Lord, have mercy upon us.

Let us pray.

O God, who (*on this day*) taught the hearts of your faithful people by sending to them the light of your Holy Spirit: Grant us by the same Spirit to have a right judgment in all things, and evermore to rejoice in his holy comfort; through Jesus Christ your Son our Lord, who lives and reigns with you, in the unity of the Holy Spirit, one God, for ever and ever. *Amen.*

Almighty God, to you all hearts are open, all desires known, and from you no secrets are hid: Cleanse the thoughts of our hearts the the inspiration of your Holy Spirit, that we may perfectly love you, and worthily magnify your holy Name; through Christ our Lord. *Amen.*

Almighty and everlasting God, by whose Spirit the whole body of your faithful people is governed and sanctified: Receive our supplications and prayers, which we offer before you for all members of your holy Church, that in their vocation and ministry they may truly and devoutly serve you; through our Lord and Savior Jesus Christ, who lives and reigns with you, in the unity of the Holy Spirit, one God, now and for ever. *Amen.*

THE CUDDESDON COLLEGE OFFICE BOOK
AND THE BOOK OF COMMON PRAYER 1979

•87 Come, Holy Spirit

Come Spirit of wisdom, and teach us to value the highest gifts.
Come, Holy Spirit.

Come, Spirit of understanding, and show us all things in the light of eternity.
Come, Holy Spirit.

Come, Spirit of counsel, and guide us along the straight and narrow path to our heavenly home.
Come, Holy Spirit.

Come, Spirit of might, and strengthen us against every evil spirit and interest which would separate us from you.
Come, Holy Spirit.

Come, Spirit of knowledge, and teach us the shortness of life and the length of eternity.
Come, Holy Spirit.

Come, Spirit of godliness, and stir up our minds and hearts to love and serve the Lord our God all our days.
Come, Holy Spirit.

Come, Spirit of the fear of the Lord, and make us tremble with awe and reverence before your divine majesty.
Come, Holy Spirit.

Holy Father,
in loving gratitude for all that you have accomplished for our salvation
    through Jesus Christ our Lord,
we pray for the fullness of the gifts of the Holy Spirit:
That we may praise you as we ought,
even with sighs and groans unutterable,
as we await the full outcome of your divine purposes;
for you indeed are God and we glorify you,
Father, Son and Holy Spirit,
now and for ever. Amen.

PRAISE HIM!

•88 Sunday

This is the day which the Lord hath made:
Let us be glad and rejoice in it.

This is the day he hath sanctified to himself, and called by his own most
holy Name:
Let us be glad and rejoice in it.

That in it we may meet to adore his greatness, and admire the wonders of his
infinite power:
Let us be glad and rejoice in it.

That we may remember his innumerable mercies, and deeply imprint them in
our hearts:
Let us be glad and rejoice in it.

That we may visit his holy temple, and humbly present our homage at his
altar:
Let us be glad and rejoice in it.

That sacred altar, where the sacrifice of the Lamb of God is shown forth, and
the memory of our Savior's love continually renewed.
This is the day which the Lord hath made;
Let us be glad and rejoice in it.

JOHN WESLEY

•89 A Litany for Sunday

Jesus, who on this day of the week rose from the dead:
Have mercy on us.

Jesus, who on this same day put on life immortal:
Have mercy on us.

Jesus, who on this same day appeared to Mary Magdalene and to the
Apostles:
Have mercy on us.

Jesus, who on this same day opened the eyes of the two disciples going to
Emmaus:
Have mercy on us.

Jesus, who on this same day comforted your Apostles, and gave them peace:
Have mercy on us.

Jesus, who on this same day confirmed your Apostles in the faith of the Resurrection, by showing them your hands and your feet:
Have mercy on us.

Jesus, who on this same day breathed on the Apostles and gave them the Holy Spirit:
Have mercy on us.

Jesus, who on this same day opened their understanding to know the Scriptures:
Have mercy on us.

Jesus, who on this same day gave them power to remit sins:
Have mercy on us.

Jesus, who on this same day sent the Apostles on their mission, and commanded them to go and teach all nations:
Have mercy on us.

Jesus, who on a Sunday condescended to the weakness of St. Thomas, and by the evidence of your sacred wounds healed his unbelief:
Have mercy on us.

Jesus, who on a Sunday sent down the Holy Spirit on the Apostles, and thus prepared them for laying the foundation of your Church:
Have mercy on us.

Jesus, who on a Sunday moved your Apostle Peter to preach the first Christian sermon to his fellow Jews:
Have mercy on us.

Jesus, who on this Sunday is present among us now in Word and Sacrament to heal and forgive and empower:
Have mercy on us.

Jesus, who on this Sunday gives us a vision of heaven and a foretaste of everlasting life:
Have mercy on us, now and always. Amen.

KYRIE ELEISON

Saints and Commemorations

•90 Litany of the Saints

God the Father in heaven: *Have mercy on us.*
God the Son, Redeemer of the world: *Have mercy on us.*
God the Holy Spirit: *Have mercy on us.*
Holy Trinity, one God: *Have mercy on us.*

For all the following, the response is "Pray for us."

> Mary and Joseph:
> Peter and Paul:
> Thomas and Andrew:
> James and John:
> Matthew, Mark and Luke:
> Mary and Martha and Mary Magdalene:
> Barnabas and Timothy:
>
> Stephen, the first of the martyrs:
> Polycarp and Ignatius:
> Justin and Hippolytus:
> Agnes, Perpetua and Felicity:
> Lawrence and Cyprian:
> Thomas Becket and Thomas More:
> Jan Hus and William Tyndale:
> Dietrich Bonhoeffer and Martin Luther King:
> Camillo Torres and Janani Luwum:
> Ambrose and Jerome:

Leo and Gregory:
Athanasius and Augustine of Hippo:
Basil of Caesarea and John Chrysostom:
Martin of Tours and Nicolas of Myra:
Catherine, Monica and Elizabeth of Hungary:
Columba and David:
Patrick and Brigid:
Cyril and Methodius:
Augustine of Canterbury and Boniface:
Ignatius Loyola and Francis Xavier:
John Carroll and Samuel Seabury:
Thomas Coke and Francis Asbury:
Roger Williams and Alexander Campbell:
William Carey and Adoniram Judson:
David Livingstone and Albert Schweitzer:

Antony, Benedict and Scholastica:
Francis, Clare and Dominic:
Bernard of Clairvaux and Thomas Aquinas:
Theresa of Avila and John of the Cross:
Martin de Porres and Jean-Baptiste Vianney:
Martin Luther and John Calvin:
Cranmer, Latimer and Ridley:
George Fox and John Bunyan:
John and Charles Wesley:
George Whitefield and Jonathan Edwards:
Nathan Söderblom and John XXIII:

Dürer, Michelangelo and Palestrina:
John Donne and George Herbert:
Isaac Watts and T.S. Eliot:
Philip Nicolai and Paul Gerhardt:
Catherine Winkworth and John Mason Neale:
Bach, Schütz and Handel:
Florence Nightingale and Elizabeth Seton:
Dag Hammarskjöld and C.S. Lewis:
All holy men and women:
All our brothers and sisters who now rest in the Lord:

We remember with thanksgiving and praise, O Lord, all of your faithful servants who throughout the long centuries have witnessed to your Name: the mighty and the lowly, great leaders and humble men and women, those who have served you amid prosperity and those who in the day of trouble have not failed, those in foreign places and those in this land.
Father of us all,

make us ever aware of the presence of this great company.
Grant that we may find,
in the reality of your nearness,
in the nearness of those countless other servants
who are separated from us by years and distance.
As we join our worship and labor to theirs,
may we know ourselves to be part of that great cloud of witnesses.
And so may all your people be united in faith,
that your Church may live to serve and praise you
in the one unbroken fellowship of your love,
through our Lord and Savior, Jesus Christ. Amen.

ADAPTED BY JEFFERY W. ROWTHORN*

•91 Invocation of the Saints

This may be led by two voices.

1: Bridegroom of poverty, our brother Francis, follower of Jesus and friend of creation:
Stand here beside us.

2: Apostle of nonviolence, Gandhi the Mahatma, reproach to the churches:
Stand here beside us.

1: John XXIII, Pope and friend of the poor, who longed for the unity of all people:
Stand here beside us.

2: Peacemakers in the world, Dag Hammarskjöld and Desmond Tutu, called children of God:
Stand here beside us.

1: Mask of the Christ, Gautama the Buddha, and Mother Teresa, fountains of compassion:
Stand here beside us.

2: Harriet Tubman and Frederick Douglass, and all fighters for freedom:
Stand here beside us.

1: Madman in America, Johnny Appleseed, planter of Eden:
Stand here beside us.

2: Visionary and apostle, John of Patmos, resisting the Beast:
Stand here beside us.

1: Visionaries and poets, Caedmon, Dante, William Blake, John Bunyan and Isaac Watts, pilgrims of the inner light:
Stand here beside us.

2: Faithful harlot, Mary Magdalene, first witness of the new life:
Stand here beside us.

1: Johann Sebastian Bach, Wolfgang Amadeus Mozart, Ludwig van Beethoven, and all who speak the soul's language:
Stand here beside us.

2: Students of the earth, Charles Darwin, Pierre Teilhard de Chardin and Margaret Mead, voyagers in the past and in the future:
Stand here beside us.

1: Children of the synagogue, Albert Einstein, Karl Marx, and Sigmund Freud, divers in the sea of humanity:
Stand here beside us.

2: Witnesses in England, John and Charles Wesley, street ministers:
Stand here beside us.

1: Reformers and leaders of protest, Amos of Tekoa, Paul of Tarsus, Jan Hus, Martin Luther, and all your companions:
Stand here beside us.

2: Menno Simons and George Fox, explorers in the Gospel:
Stand here beside us.

1: Confessors in chains, Dietrich Bonhoeffer, and the Berrigan brothers, war resisters:
Stand here beside us.

2: Confessor in Africa, Augustine of Hippo, city-planner for God's people:
Stand here beside us.

1: Confessor in Russia, Boris Pasternak, poet of reconciliation:
Stand here beside us.

2: Confessors in America, Henry David Thoreau, Robert Frost and Thomas Merton, hermits and free thinkers:
Stand here beside us.

1: Innocents of Guernica, Sharpeville, and Birmingham, and all victims of lynching, in your undeserved deaths:
Stand here beside us.

2: Innocents of Coventry, Dresden, Tokyo, and all victims of bombing, caught up in a sea of fire:
Stand here beside us.

1:   Innocents of Hiroshima and Nagasaki, pierced by needles of flame:
Stand here beside us.

2:   Innocents of Auschwitz, Dachau, and all concentration camps, in your despair and dying:
Stand here beside us.

1:   Innocents of Biafra and Armenia, objects of genocide:
Stand here beside us.

2:   Innocents of Wounded Knee and Mylai, God's wheat ground in the mill of war:
Stand here beside us.

1:   Martyrs of Africa: Perpetua, mother; Felicity, slave; and all your companions:
Stand here beside us.

2:   Martyrs and confessors, Polycarp, Ignatius, and Justin, who refused to offer incense to Caesar:
Stand here beside us.

1:   Martyr in England, Thomas Cranmer, and all who died to renew the Church:
Stand here beside us.

2:   Martyr in Columbia, Camillo Torres, priest and revolutionary:
Stand here beside us.

1:   Martyrs of Kent State, witnesses to the hopes of the young:
Stand here beside us.

2:   Martyr for America, Martin Luther King, organizer for peace and justice:
Stand here beside us.

1:   Unwed mother, blessed Mary, fair wellspring of our liberation:
Stand here beside us.

2:   Our leader and Lord, Jesus the Son of God, bright cornerstone of our unity in a new Spirit:
Stand here beside us.

1:   Almighty God, you have surrounded us with a great cloud of witnesses: Grant that we, encouraged by the good example of these your servants, may persevere in running the race that is set before us, until at last, with all your saints attain to your eternal joy; through Jesus Christ, the pioneer and perfecter of our faith, who lives and reigns with you and the Holy Spirit, one God, for ever and ever. *Amen.*

THE COVENANT OF PEACE

•92 A Great Cloud of Witnesses

We give thanks to you, O Lord our God, for all your servants and witnesses of time past.

For Abraham, the father of believers, and Sarah his wife:
We give you thanks, O Lord.

For Moses, the lawgiver, and Aaron, the priest:
We give you thanks, O Lord.

For Miriam and Joshua, Deborah and Gideon:
We give you thanks, O Lord.

For Samuel with Hannah his mother:
We give you thanks, O Lord.

For Isaiah and all the prophets:
We give you thanks, O Lord.

For Mary, the mother of our Lord:
We give you thanks, O Lord.

For Peter and Paul and all the apostles:
We give you thanks, O Lord.

For Mary and Martha, and Mary Magdalene:
We give you thanks, O Lord.

For Stephen, the first martyr:
We give you thanks, O Lord.

For all the martyrs and saints in every age and in every land:
We give you thanks, O Lord.

In your mercy, O Lord our God, give us, as you gave to them, the hope of salvation and the promise of eternal life; through Jesus Christ our Lord, the first-born of many from the dead. *Amen.*

THE BOOK OF COMMON PRAYER 1979

•93 All Saints

Presiding Minister:

Throughout the ages men and women have followed Jesus. We pray that we may walk in their footsteps.

Silence

Leader:
That our bishops, pastors, and teachers may show forth the spirit of the apostles so that their message will have the power to convince those who hear their words, we pray to the Lord.
Lord, hear our prayer.

For people who are laughed at or discriminated against or persecuted for trying to live like Christians, that they may have strength to persevere like the martyrs, we pray to the Lord.
Lord, hear our prayer.

That the leaders of our nation and other nations may have the wisdom and compassion of the saints who in their day were kings and chancellors and peacemakers, we pray to the Lord.
Lord, hear our prayer.

That those who drop out of our society may have the longing for God, the gentleness and purity of the holy hermits and pilgrims who went before them, we pray to the Lord.
Lord, hear our prayer.

May all of us follow with joy and simplicity the great throng of men and women who have gone before us with steady strides, or stumbling and wandering but finding their way back to him who is the Way. For this we pray to the Lord.
Lord, hear our prayer.

Presiding Minister:
Lord, we thank you for this feast of all your friends, and we ask that we may be in that number when the saints come marching in. *Amen.*

PRAYERS OF THE FAITHFUL

• 94 Litany of Commemoration

Almighty and everlasting God, before whom stand the spirits of the living and the dead, for all who have witnessed a good confession for your glory and the welfare of the world; for patriarchs, prophets, and apostles; for the wise of every land and nation, and for all teachers of your people on earth: *We praise you, O God, and bless your Name.*

For the martyrs of the holy faith, the faithful witnesses to Christ of whom the world was not worthy, and for all who have resisted falsehood and wrong unto suffering or death:
We praise you, O God, and bless your Name.

For all who have labored and suffered for freedom, good government, just laws, and the sanctity of the home, and for all who have given their lives for their country:
We praise you, O God, and bless your Name.

For all who have sought to bless us by their service and life, and to lighten the dark places of the earth:
We praise you, O God, and bless your Name.

For those who have been tender and true and brave in all times and places, and for all who have been one with you in the communion of Christ's Spirit and in the strength of his love:
We praise you, O God, and bless your Name.

For the dear friends and kindred whose faces we see no more, but whose love is with us for ever:
We praise you, O God, and bless your Name.

For the teachers and companions of our childhood and youth, and the members of our household of faith who worship you now in heaven:
We praise you, O God, and bless your Name.

For the grace which was given to all these, and for the trust and hope in which they lived and died:
We praise you, O God, and bless your Name.

That we may hold them in continual remembrance and that the sanctity of their wisdom and goodness may rest upon our earthly days:
We entreat you to hear us, O God.

That we may ever think of them as with you, and be sure that where they are, there we may be also:
We entreat you to hear us, O God.

That we may have a hope beyond this world for all your children, and that we may be comforted and sustained by the promise of a time when none shall be a stranger and an exile from your kingdom and household:
We entreat you to hear us, O God.

In the communion of the Holy Spirit, with the faithful and the saintly in heaven, with the redeemed of every age, with our beloved who dwell in your presence and peace, we, who still fight and suffer on earth, unite in ascribing thanksgiving, glory, honor, and power to you, O Lord our God.
Glory to the Father, and to the Son, and to the Holy Spirit:

as it was in the beginning, is now, and will be for ever. Amen.

WILLARD SPERRY
–WITH ONE VOICE

•95 Litany of the Virgin Mary

O Mary, kind and gentle maid:
Give help to us.

O casket of the Lord's body, O shrine of mysteries:
Pray for us that through thee our transgressions may be forgiven.

O compassionate and forgiving one:
Entreat with us the true-judging King, thy fair fragrant child.

O fair and bright ark of gold, O Mother of righteousness:
Pray with us thy First-born to save us at the judgment.

O Lady victorious, long-descended, host-attended:
Entreat with us the mighty Christ, thy Father and thy Son.

O city fair and fragrant whom the King did choose:
Be thou our protection.

O royal door elect, through which God came into the world:
Be thou our protection.

For the sake of the fair birth which was conceived in thy womb:
Be thou our protection.

For the sake of the Only-begotten who is high King in every place:
Be thou our protection.

For the sake of his Cross, which is above every cross:
Be thou our protection.

For the sake of his Resurrection who arose before all:
Be thou our protection.

For the sake of his holy household drawn from every place:
Be thou our protection.

O Mary, be thou our protection in the Kingdom of fair safety:
That we may go with Jesus, we pray, while life lasts. Amen.

IRISH LITANIES*

•96 Song of the Blessed Virgin Mary

Hail, Mary:
Full of grace; the Lord is with you.

My being proclaims the greatness of the Lord,
   my spirit finds joy in God my Savior.
For he has looked upon his servant in her lowliness;
   all ages to come shall call me blessed.

Hail, Mary:
Full of grace; the Lord is with you.

God who is mighty has done great things for me,
   holy is his name;
His mercy is from age to age
   on those who fear him.

Hail, Mary:
Full of grace; the Lord is with you.

He has shown might with his arm,
   he has confused the proud in their inmost thoughts.
He has deposed the mighty from their thrones
   and raised the lowly to high places.
The hungry he has given every good thing,
   while the rich he has sent empty away.

Hail, Mary:
Full of grace; the Lord is with you.

He has upheld Israel his servant,
   ever mindful of his mercy;
Even as he promised our fathers,
   promised Abraham and his descendants forever.

Hail, Mary:
Full of grace; the Lord is with you.

The following Doxology may be sung or said:

Glory be to God the Father;
Glory be to God the Son;
Glory be to God the Spirit;
Glory to the Three in One!
From the heart of blessed Mary,
From all saints the song ascends,
And the Church the strain reechoes
Unto earth's remotest ends. Amen.

LUKE 1:46-55 (NEW AMERICAN BIBLE)
–HYMN STANZA BY ROLAND F. PALMER*

• 97 St. Joseph, Husband of Mary

As a congregation gathered with Joseph's own humble trust and hope in the Spirit, let us pray to the Lord.

Silence

For this community, that a man may work here with dignity at a trade he loves, support and shelter his family, and live to see his children and his children's children find peace and fulfillment in this world, let us pray to the Lord.
Lord, hear our prayer.

For the Church, that free men may labor here as brothers, as among equals, vibrant with the life and strength of the Kingdom begun here by Christ, let us pray to the Lord.
Lord, hear our prayer.

For all who have been deprived of their fathers and their fathers' work, through slavery, starvation, abandonment, and annihilation, let us pray to the Lord.
Lord, hear our prayer.

For foster parents and parents by adoption, that they will find true happiness in the mystery of parenthood which they share with St. Joseph, let us pray to the Lord.
Lord, hear our prayer.

For us, that we might let the Spirit of peace enter our lives and commit ourselves to a new vision of the human community, let us pray to the Lord.
Lord, hear our prayer.

Silence

Father, give to all men the strength you gave to Joseph to do your will when he did not understand it. Help us trust in your Word as he trusted in your Spirit; may we thus share with Christ in making the world your Kingdom on earth. *Amen.*

PRAYERS OF THE FAITHFUL

•98 St. Paul

Almighty and ever-blessed God, you have not at any time left yourself without witnesses on earth, but have in every age raised up saintly and prophetic spirits to lead us into the way of faith and love. We praise your name for the gift of your holy apostle, Saint Paul. And we thank you for the zeal with which you endowed him to carry to our western world that lamp of truth which you had so lately lit in an eastern land.

Saint Paul said, "Let all bitterness, and wrath, and anger, and clamor, and all evil speaking, be put away from you, with all malice: and be kind to one another, tender-hearted, forgiving one another, even as God for Christ's sake has forgiven you."
O God, incline our hearts to follow in this way.

Saint Paul said, "Put on the Lord Jesus Christ, and make no provision for the flesh, to fulfill the lusts thereof."
O God, incline our hearts to follow in this way.

Saint Paul said, "I keep my body under, and bring it into subjection."
O God, incline our hearts to follow in this way.

Saint Paul said, "Let nothing be done through strife or vainglory; but in lowliness of mind let each esteem others better than themselves."
O God, incline our hearts to follow in this way.

Saint Paul said, "Those that glory, let them glory in the Lord."
O God, incline our hearts to follow in this way.

Saint Paul said, "Pray at all times in the Spirit, with all prayer and supplication. To that end keep alert with all perseverance, making supplication for all the saints, and also for me, that utterance may be given me in opening my mouth boldly to proclaim the mystery of the Gospel."
O God, we pray today especially for all who,
following in the footsteps of Saint Paul,
are now laboring to bring the light of Christ's Gospel to distant lands.
Amen.

JOHN BAILLIE

•99 St. John the Baptist

O God, our Father, help us in everything to follow the example of your servant John the Baptist.
Help us sincerely to repent.

Show us the ugliness and the evil of our lives;
Show us the harm we have done,
    and the heartbreak that we have caused;
Show us how we have shamed ourselves, disappointed
    those who love us, and grieved you.
Make us truly sorry for all our sins and our mistakes,
    and help us to show our sorrow by living better in the days to come.
Help us like John constantly to speak the truth.
Keep us from twisting the truth to conceal our own
    faults;
Keep us from evading the truth we do not wish to see;
Keep us from silencing the truth, because we are more afraid to offend
    our fellows than we are to disobey you;
Save us from speaking or from acting a lie,
    and save us from false words and from cowardly
    silence.
Help us like John boldly to rebuke vice.
Keep us from being censorious or arrogant, self-
    righteous or fault-finding;
But help us never to be silent
    in the presence of injustice or impurity;
Grant that we may never see another drifting or rushing
    to disaster without speaking the word of warning we ought to speak in
    love.
Help us like John patiently to suffer for the truth
Grant that we may set allegiance to the truth above all
    worldly success;
Grant that we may be ready to face loneliness and un-
    popularity for the sake of the truth;
Grant that we may follow the truth wherever it leads,
    that we may obey the truth whatever it demands, that
    we may speak the truth whatever it costs.
So grant that living the truth we may be the true servants of you who are the
God of truth; through Jesus Christ our Lord. Amen.

WILLIAM BARCLAY
–PRAYERS FOR THE CHRISTIAN YEAR

• 100 Feast of the Transfiguration

Loving Father, you transfigured your beloved Son and revealed the Holy
Spirit in the bright cloud: Enable us to hear the Word of Christ with faithful
hearts.
Kyrie eleison.

Loving Father, you made light to rise in the darkness, and you have shone in
our hearts, to make known your glory in the face of Jesus Christ: Revive in
us the spirit of contemplation.
Kyrie eleison.

O Christ, you took your friends with you and led them to a high mountain:
May your Church stay close to you, in the peace and hope of your glory.
Kyrie eleison.

O Christ, by your Transfiguration you revealed the Resurrection to your
disciples before your Passion began; we pray for the Church in all the
difficulties of this world; in our trials may we be transfigured by the joy of
your victory.
Kyrie eleison.

O Christ, you led Peter, James, and John down from the mountain and into
the suffering world; when our hearts crave permanence, may we know the
permanence of your love as you take us with you on your way.
Kyrie eleison.

O Christ, you will transfigure our poor bodies and conform them to your
glorious body; we pray to you for our brothers and sisters who are dying;
may they be changed into your likeness, from glory to glory.
Kyrie eleison.

The Lord be with you,
And also with you.
Let us pray.

Silence

O God, whose face we cannot see, you have made known your love by the
lives of faithful witnesses. We give you thanks for the revelation of your
glory in the face of our Lord Jesus Christ, for your confirmation of his
disciples and for the promise of his victory. May the light of your presence
shine on your People, that all may see the fulfillment of their hopes in the
coming of our Savior, Jesus Christ. *Amen.*

Lord Jesus Christ, light shining in our darkness,
have mercy on our tired and doubting hearts.
Renew in us the courage we need,

that we may bring to completion the work your calling has begun in us.
Freely you gave your life on the Cross,
freely you took it again in your Resurrection,
for you live and reign now and for ever. Amen.

PRAISE GOD: COMMON PRAYER AT TAIZÉ

• 101 Reformation Sunday

Let us celebrate the lives and legacy of our spiritual forebears, the Protestant Reformers.
They lived and died long ago, but are alive with God and in the Church.

We thank you, Lord, for the forerunners: for Peter Waldo, John Wycliffe, and John Hus.
They fought lonely fights and died lonely deaths, but their sacrifice was not in vain.

We thank you for your servant Martin Luther:
For his experience of your grace, his love of music and family, his glorious stubbornness.

We thank you for your servant John Calvin:
For his giant intellect, his pastoral faithfulness, his insistence upon the social dimension of the Gospel.

We thank you for your servant John Knox:
For his rough-hewn courage, his tireless striving, his eventual success in bringing an entire nation under the sway of your Word.

We thank you for your servant Thomas Cranmer:
For his way with words, his legacy of common prayer, and his gift to us of worship in our mother tongue.

We reaffirm, O Lord, the Reformers' commitment to the supremacy of the Scriptures.
Help us to spend more time in the study of your Word.

We reaffirm their commitment to the weekly celebration of the Lord's Supper.
Help us to gather with regularity around your Table.

We reaffirm their commitment to one, and only one, Mediator between you and us.
Help us to engage in prayer to you more frequently and more honestly.

We reaffirm the Reformers' commitment to justification by faith.

Help us to find new ways to serve you in our relations with others.

We reaffirm their commitment to liberty of conscience.
Help us to be more responsible in using our civil and religious freedoms.

We pray, Lord, that we may be positive Protestants: *Christians*
Not just protesting against wrongs, but witnessing for the Good News of your love.

We pray that ancient grudges may be buried and forgotten:
And that, in this new day, we may unite with all our fellow-Christians in common, ongoing reformation.

This is our deepest plea, Lord:
That the reforming of your Church may continue, beginning with us, with each of us, with all of us. Amen.

MODELS FOR MINISTERS I*

•102 The Last Sunday of the Year

O God our Father, as this year comes to an end, we remember before you all its days.

Every happy hour and every happy day;
Every new thing we have learned and seen and done;
Every new friend we have made, and the old friends to whom we are closer
   now than ever we were:
We remember and give thanks with joy.

Everything which was difficult to face or hard to bear,
   but out of which we came, wiser in mind and stronger in character;
Every failure and disappointment that has kept us humble;
Everything that has shown us how dangerous life can be,
   and how much we need you:
We remember and give thanks with joy.

Every task in which we failed;
Every temptation to which we succumbed;
Every person we hurt and failed and disappointed;
Every word and deed for which we are sorry now:
We remember and confess with sorrow.

All those for whom this has been a thrilling, an exciting, and a successful year:
That they may remember to give you thanks;

All those for whom this has been a sad year, and who come to the end of it lonelier than they were at its beginning:
That they may find comfort and courage to go on;

All those for whom this has been an ordinary year, when othing special seemed to happen, making them forget that it is in life's routine they win or lose their destiny:
That they may know themselves to be blessed by you.

And help us now, made wise by the lessons life has taught us, to go on to higher achievements and nobler things, through Jesus Christ our Lord. *Amen.*

WILLIAM BARCLAY
–EPILOGUES AND PRAYERS

•103 A New Year's Litany

O God, who inhabits eternity, whose name is holy, with hushed spirits in the quiet of thy sanctuary we wait the closing moment of another year.
We lift up our hearts to thee, O Lord.

From the failures of the past, from broken hopes and disappointed ambitions, from our sins against ourselves and against others, and from the transiency and vicissitude of our lives:
We lift up our hearts to thee, O Lord.

We confess the unworthy living that has stained the record of the year that now is dying. For pardon, for grace to make restitution, for a clean heart and a right spirit with which to enter the new year:
We lift up our hearts to thee, O Lord.

Grant us honesty to face ourselves before we confront another year. Save us from self-deceit, mean excuses, unworthy evasions, and prepare us with inner integrity and spiritual resource, that we may be adequate for all that lies before us.
Lord, have mercy upon us and grant us this blessing.

From loss of faith and hope and courage, from anxiety that harasses us, fear that affrights us, cowardice that defeats us, and from the loss of thy companionship, without which no life is good, no soul is strong:
Good Lord, deliver us.

From cherishing ill will in a world that perishes for want of good will, from selfishness in a world whose need of generosity and magnaninmity is deep and desperate, from so living that Christ shall be crucified again and the Kingdom of God delay its coming:

Good Lord, deliver us.

Confirm now in each of us some worthy decision. Bring us to the new year's beginning with such vision of our duty, such resolution to perform it, and such resources for its consummation that, whether in the year ahead we live or fall asleep, we shall be neither dishonored nor ashamed before thee. *Lord, have mercy upon us and grant us this blessing. Amen.*

HARRY EMERSON FOSDICK

Dedications and Anniversaries

•104 In Thanksgiving for a Church

This Litany may also be used on the anniversary of the dedication or consecration of a church, or on other suitable occasions.

Let us thank God whom we worship here in the beauty of holiness.

Eternal God, the heaven of heavens cannot contain you, much less the walls of temples made with hands. Graciously receive our thanks for this place, and accept the work of our hands, offered to your honor and glory.

For the Church universal, of which these visible buildings are the symbol:
We thank you, Lord.

For your presence whenever two or three have gathered together in your Name:
We thank you, Lord.

For this place where we may be still and know that you are God:
We thank you, Lord.

For making us your children by adoption and grace, and refreshing us day by day with the bread of life:
We thank you, Lord.

For the knowledge of your will and the grace to perform it:
We thank you, Lord.

For the fulfilling of our desires and petitions as you see best for us:
We thank you, Lord.

For the pardon of our sins, which restores us to the company of your faithful people:
We thank you, Lord.

For the blessing of our vows and the crowning of our years with your goodness:
We thank you, Lord.

For the faith of those who have gone before us and for our encouragement by their perseverance:
We thank you, Lord.

For the fellowship of [_____, our patron, and of] all your Saints:
We thank you, Lord.

Silence. The Litany concludes with the following Doxology.

Yours, O Lord, is the greatness, the power, the glory, the victory, and the majesty:
For everything in heaven and on earth is yours.
Yours, O Lord, is the kingdom:
And you are exalted as head over all. Amen.

THE BOOK OF COMMON PRAYER 1979

•105 On the Anniversary of a Church

For those whose faith, courage, and Christian conviction and whose diligent effort and financial sacrifice resulted in the building of this house of worship:
We thank you, O God.

For those who labored with mind and hand to design and construct this sanctuary that Christian people might worship the Lord in the beauty of holiness:
We thank you, O God.

For all those servants of God who have led your people in worship here, who have preached your word from this pulpit, and who have administered the sacraments to waiting and believing hearts:
We thank you, O God.

For all those who have come to this place seeking you, and who, in worshiping you in spirit and in truth, have found you:
We thank you, O God.

For those who have brought their children here for Christian baptism, for those who have pledged their love to one another at this holy altar, and for

those who in Christian faith and trust have here parted with loved ones and committed them to your love and care:
We thank you, O God.

For all those who have here confessed their faith in Jesus Christ, have shared in the life and witness of the Church, and committed themselves to the Christian life:
We thank you, O God.

For sins that have been confessed and forgiven here, for burdens that have been made easier to carry, for distressed and troubled hearts that have known the peace that passes all understanding, and for lives that have been inspired to new heights of love and of service:
We thank you, O God.

For all your goodness and love revealed to us in this house of worship, we praise you and we thank you, O God. Amen.

ERNEST O. GEIGIS
–WORSHIP SERVICES FOR SPECIAL OCCASIONS

• 106 The Dedication of a New Church

The Leaders of the Congregation say:

We present this building to be dedicated to the glory of God and the service of humanity.

The Minister asks:

By what name shall this church henceforth be known?

Answer:

It shall be called ＿＿＿.

The Minister says:

Beloved in the Lord, we rejoice that God put it into the hearts of his people to build this house to the glory of his name. Let us now dedicate it and set it apart for the worship of Almighty God and the service of all his people.

To the glory of God the Father, who has called us by his grace:
We dedicate this house.

To the honor of his Son, who loved us and gave himself for us:
We dedicate this house.

To the praise of the Holy Spirit, who illumines and sanctifies us:

We dedicate this house.

For the worship of God in prayer and praise,
For the preaching of the everlasting Gospel,
For the celebration of the holy Sacraments:
We dedicate this house.

For comfort to all who mourn,
For strength to those who are tempted,
For light to those who seek the way:
We dedicate this house.

For the hallowing of family life,
For the teaching and guiding of the young,
For the perfecting of the saints:
We dedicate this house.

For the conversion of sinners,
For the promotion of righteousness,
For the extension of the Kingdom of God:
We dedicate this house.

In the unity of the faith,
In the bond of Christian fellowship,
In charity and good will to all:
We dedicate this house.

In gratitude for the labors of all who love and serve this church,
In loving remembrance of those who have finished their course,
In the hope of everlasting life through Jesus Christ, our Lord:
We dedicate this house.

We, the people of this church,
being compassed about with so great a cloud of witnesses,
grateful for our heritage,
sensible of the sacrifice of our forebears in the faith,
and confessing that apart from us their work cannot be made
    perfect,
now dedicate ourselves anew to the worship and service of
    Almighty God;
through Jesus Christ our Lord. Amen.

Minister:

Accept, O God our Father, this service at our hands, and bless it to the end
that this congregation of faithful people may show forth in their lives your
love and your truth; and grant that this house may be the place where your

honor dwells and the whole earth be filled with your glory; through Jesus Christ our Lord. *Amen.*

EARL S. WALKER
–WORSHIP SERVICES FOR SPECIAL OCCASIONS

• 107 The Setting Apart of an Altar

The Bishop says

Let us now pray for the setting apart of the Altar.

The Bishop goes to the Table and, with arms extended, says

We praise you, Almighty and eternal God, that for us and for our salvation, you sent your Son Jesus Christ to be born among us, that through him we might become your sons and daughters.
Blessed be your Name, Lord God.

We praise you for his life on earth, and for his death upon the Cross, through which he offered himself as a perfect sacrifice.
Blessed be your Name, Lord God.

We praise you for raising him from the dead, and for exalting him to be our great High Priest.
Blessed be your Name, Lord God.

We praise you for sending your Holy Spirit to make us holy, and to unite us in your holy Church.
Blessed be your Name, Lord God.

The Bishop lays a hand upon the Table, and continues:

Lord God, hear us. Sanctify this Table dedicated to you. Let it be to us a sign of the heavenly Altar where your saints and angels praise you for ever. Accept here the continual recalling of the sacrifice of your Son. Grant that all who eat and drink at this holy Table may be fed and refreshed by his flesh and blood, be forgiven for their sins, united with one another, and strengthened for your service.
Blessed be your Name, Father, Son, and Holy Spirit; now and for endless ages. Amen.

(Members of the congregation vest the Altar, place the vessels on it, and light the candles. The Eucharist is then celebrated, with the Bishop as the principal Celebrant.)

THE BOOK OF COMMON PRAYER 1979

•108 In Thanksgiving for the Bible

O God, this day we thank you for your Book.
> For those who wrote it, for those who lived close to you, so that you
> could speak to them and so give them a message for their day and for
> ours;
> *We thank you, O God.*

> For those who translated it into our own languages, often at the cost of
> blood and sweat and agony and death, so that your word can speak to
> us in the tongue we know;
> *We thank you, O God.*

> For scholars whose devoted and consecrated study and toil has opened the
> meaning of your Book to others;
> *We thank you, O God.*

> For those who print it and publish it, and for the great Bible Societies
> whose work makes it possible for the poorest of people all over the
> world to possess your word;
> *We thank you, O God.*

> For its thrilling stories of high and gallant adventure;
> For its poetry which lingers for ever in the memory;
> For its teaching about how to live and how to act and how to speak;
> For its record of the thoughts of women and men about you and about our
> blessed Lord;
> For its comfort in sorrow, for its guidance in perplexity, for its hope in
> despair;
> Above all else for its picture of Jesus:
> *We thank you, O God.*

Make us at all times
> *Constant in reading it:*
> *Glad to listen to it;*
> *Eager to study it;*
> *Retentive to remember it;*
> *Resolute to obey it.*

And so grant that in searching the Scriptures we may find life for ourselves
and for others; through Jesus Christ our Lord. *Amen.*

WILLIAM BARCLAY
–PRAYERS FOR THE CHRISTIAN YEAR

•109 The Dedication of a Bible

In honor of God our Heavenly Father who created us and gave us the priceless gift of speech:
We dedicate this Bible.

In praise of Jesus Christ, the Incarnate Word, who spoke with matchless power and grace:
We dedicate this Bible.

In remembrance of the Holy Spirit, who speaks to the hidden things in our hearts:
We dedicate this Bible.

In celebration of all those who were inspired to write and to translate the sacred scriptures:
We dedicate this Bible.

So that we may continue to hear the story of God's love and Christ's redemptive sacrifice:
We dedicate this Bible.

So that our children may come to know the life of Christ and understand his message:
We dedicate this Bible.

So that our young people may receive direction, comfort, and counsel from the treasure-store of our faith:
We dedicate this Bible.

So that we may all have the comforting assurance of pardon and forgiveness, and be encouraged to walk in newness of life:
We dedicate this Bible.

To the glory of God, the enlightening of this congregation, and the strengthening of the ties which bind us to people everywhere, this Bible is now dedicated. May humble tongues proclaim its undying truths and receptive hearts receive the message it imparts. *Amen.*

Almighty God, you have spoken to us through your Holy Word; we thank you for this Bible and ask you to bless and sanctify its use.
May all who read from it in the appointed services of our church, and all who hear it, receive the fullest blessing of your love.
May its eternal message serve as a lamp to our feet as we travel through darkened places.
May its inspiration lift us when we feel discouraged and downtrodden.
May it illumine our lives with the light of the life of our Lord Jesus Christ.
In his Name we pray. Amen.

• 110 The Dedication of a New Organ

Men: Alleluia! Praise God in his holy temple;
Women: Praise God in the firmament of his power.
Men: Praise God for his mighty acts;
Women: Praise God for his excellent greatness.
Men: Praise God with the blast of the ram's horn;
Women: Praise God with lyre and harp.
Men: Praise God with timbrel and dance;
Women: Praise God with strings and pipe.
Men: Praise God with resounding cymbals;
Women: Praise God with loud-clanging cymbals.
   All: Let everything that has breath praise the Lord. Alleluia!

Leader continues

To the honor and glory of God, author of all beauty and goodness, giver of all talents and appreciation for music:
We dedicate this organ.

With faith in Jesus Christ, that he will continue to inspire men and women to offer God their best in music and song:
We dedicate this organ.

Moved by the Holy Spirit, who gives life to our worship and service of God, and guides us in the understanding of truth and beauty:
We dedicate this organ.

To aid in the healing of discord, in the uplifting of the depressed, and in the comforting of the sorrowful:
We dedicate this organ.

To support the singing of psalms and hymns and spiritual songs in such ways that men and women may go forth from this house of God joyfully renewed and determined to do God's holy will:
We dedicate this organ.

Holy and eternal God, Father, Son and Holy Ghost, to whom all the joyful companies of heaven give adoration and glory: Graciously grant that this organ may minister to the excellency of praise in your holy temple; and so bless us as we magnify you upon earth with music and the voice of melody, that hereafter we may sing the new song in the heavenly city, where you reign, almighty, all-glorious, world without end. *Amen.*

A hymn of praise, accompanied on the organ, is now sung by all.

ADAPTED BY JEFFERY ROWTHORN

•111 At the Dedication of an Organ

O magnify the Lord with me, and let us exalt his name together.
Let us enter his gates with thanksgiving and his courts with praise.

Eternal Spirit, from whom stream all things excellent in all creation, and in whose sanctuary strength and beauty dwell, we worship you. Lift up our hearts above the harsh confusions of our time, above its din and clamor, and here refresh our souls with harmony and praise.
Praise God in his sanctuary; praise him with stringed instruments and organs.

For all makers of melody, who have taught us to rejoice in song and have lifted our spirits in hymns of gratitude and praise, we thank you. Here in your sanctuary may music give our spirits wings, until above life's discords we hear the voices of the heavenly host, singing "Hallelujah! The Lord God Omnipotent reigns."
"Let everything that has breath praise the Lord. Hallelujah!"

O God of grace, grant that this instrument for praise, which we now dedicate, may minister to the strengthening of our faith. Here in your sanctuary may we be reassured that life is not all dissonance and turmoil. Here may the beauty of the Lord, our God, be upon us.
O sing to the Lord a new song; sing to the Lord, all the earth.

Upon this congregation of your people we ask your blessing. May the outward harmony, with which we worship you here, be reflected in our daily lives – in the loveliness of friendship, in generous concord, and in good will that heals our hurts and quiets our hostilities.
In psalms and hymns and spiritual songs may we sing, making melody in our hearts to the Lord.

Especially we pray that since our lives are beset with hardship and our wayward spirits find duty difficult, we may here discover also the gladness of Christian discipleship. Here may the God of hope fill us with all joy and peace in believing, until we serve the Lord with gladness and come before his presence with singing. So comfort the sorrowful, lift up the discouraged, renew the fainthearted, and teach us to say: The Lord is our strength and our song.

O come, let us sing to the Lord; let us make a joyful noise to the rock of our salvation. Let us come before his presence with thanksgiving, and make a joyful noise to him with psalms.

As we remember our Master and his first disciples, of whom it is written, "When they had sung an hymn, they went out to the Mount of Olives," we too, being strengthened by your Spirit, ask to be made ready for our difficult tomorrows. Let not our worship here be an escape from life, but a preparation for life. Here may we be so compassed about with songs of deliverance that tomorrow we may be able to do what we ought to do and to stand what we must endure.

Wait on the Lord; be of good courage, and he shall strengthen your heart. Wait, I say, on the Lord. Amen.

An organ voluntary is now played, or a hymn or anthem sung with organ accompaniment.

HARRY EMERSON FOSDICK

•112 The Dedication of New Hymnals

The congregation holds the old hymnal in their hands as they make their response.

For all people of wisdom and understanding, of vision and poetry, who have given us memorable words wherein our hearts may rejoice and our minds be lifted up to thee:
We thank thee, O Lord.

For peal of organ and lilt of song, and for consecrated men and women who through the ages have brought forth melodies that have made our hearts rejoice and our souls stir within us:
We thank thee, O Lord.

For printers and engravers, binders and publishers, through whose labors we share in the inspiration of others:
We thank thee, O Lord.

For builders of organs and those who create music to make worship our delight:
We thank thee, O Lord.

That thou didst endow thy children with gifts of music and song; for noble themes and glorious voices:
We thank thee, O Lord.

For hearts and minds that thrill to praise thee; for moments that are precious, when, for an instant, thou revealest thyself in the span of a tune; for spirits

160

awakened and deep calling unto deep; for the sound of thy still small voice
calling us to follow thee:
We thank thee, O Lord.

O Lord, how manifold are thy works. In wisdom hast thou made them all;
the whole earth is full of thy riches. *Amen.*

*Hymn: A hymn is now sung, which is to be found only in the hymnal which is being
replaced.*

*Organ Voluntary: During this voluntary the copies of the hymnal to be replaced are
collected, and copies of the new hymnal are distributed throughout the congregation.*

We are mindful, O Lord, of the blessings these books have brought to those
who through the years have sought thee in this house of prayer. We thank
thee for dead hearts quickened, for courage renewed, for comfort found, for
sin redeemed and grace bestowed through thy truth declared in these hymns.
Through them we have entered into the labors of others and have been
inspired to set forth thy love not only with our lips but in our lives, by
giving up ourselves to thy service all the days of our lives. *Amen.*

*The congregation holding the new hymnal in their hands, stresses the italicized word in
each indicated response.*

We come together as thy Church, our Father, to worship thee and to sing thy
praise. We dedicate these hymnals that by their use our worship may be
enriched through the glory of song:
*O God, **we** dedicate these hymnals.*

These are no ordinary books, our Father. Within these pages are the living
words of trust and assurance, commitment and faith. These hymnals are a
part of thy living Church; they are the vessels of thy love. We cannot use
them except as they are truly placed before thee and consecrated in thy
service:
*O God, we **dedicate** these hymnals.*

We have chosen these particular hymnals, our Father, because they remind us
of our heritage of faith, the traditions of the Church of which we are a part,
and open up for us new avenues of meaning and understanding in our
continuing search for thy truth:
*O God, we dedicate **these** hymnals.*

In the months and years to come, our Father, we will again and again open
these pages. These books will serve as a means of grace in our corporate
worship together as the Church of Jesus Christ. May their special ministry
be to lift our voices in song and bind our hearts in Christian love:
*O God, we dedicate these **hymnals**.*

O God, we dedicate these hymnals this day and rededicate ourselves to the following of thy way for all humanity as we have come to know it in Jesus Christ. May we truly persevere in that way in our lives and may the words of our mouths and the meditations of our hearts be ever acceptable in thy sight, O Lord, our strength and our redeemer. *Amen.*

Hymn: A hymn, chosen from the newly dedicated hymnal, is now sung.

WORSHIP SERVICES FOR SPECIAL OCCASIONS

•113 The Dedication of a Carillon of Bells

By the generosity of _____ these new bells have been provided to assist us in our worship of God, and to invite all who hear them to come and worship with us. It is right that we should now dedicate these bells and set them apart to the holy use for which they are designed.

To the glory of God, Author of all beauty and goodness, Giver of all skill of mind and hand:
We dedicate these bells.

In faith in our Lord Jesus Christ, who has inspired each generation to offer in his presence the best of music:
We dedicate these bells.

Moved by the Holy Spirit, our Guide in the worship of God, our Inspiration in praise, our Helper in the understanding of truth and beauty, love and service:
We dedicate these bells.

To kindle the flame of devotion and to call by their ringing voices all who hear, to worship the Father in spirit and in truth:
We dedicate these bells.

To ring in joyous affirmation when before the altar of this church a man and woman stand to pledge to each other their lifelong affection and to establish a new home where God may be glorified and his name honored:
We dedicate these bells.

To comfort the sorrowful, to cheer the faint-hearted, to bring peace and love to human hearts, and to lead all who hear in the way of eternal life:
We dedicate these bells.

To the glory of God *(and in loving memory of _____),*

We dedicate these bells.

O God, our Father, most holy and most high, to whom we have access by the one Spirit through our Lord Jesus Christ, we give you praise and honor and worship. We thank you that you have so made us that music can lift our hearts and minds to you. Grant that we and all who will hear the music of these bells may be moved to love you more, serve you better, worship, praise and pray to you more regularly, led and inspired by your Holy Spirit. This we ask in the Name of our Lord Jesus Christ. *Amen.*

Blessing and glory,
wisdom and thanksgiving,
honor and power and might
be to our God
for ever and ever. Amen.

(The newly dedicated bells are now rung.)

GRANVILLE T. WALKER
–WORSHIP SERVICES FOR SPECIAL OCCASIONS

•114 The Dedication of Annual Pledges

Leader and People

> *We give Thee but Thine own*
> *Whate'er the gift may be;*
> *All that we have is Thine alone,*
> *A trust, O Lord, from Thee.*

As you have chosen us, O God, and enriched our lives:
We offer you ourselves, our time and talents and income.

For the ministry of the Christian Gospel, the inspiration of sacred music, and the singing of hymns from every age:
We offer you ourselves, our time and talents and income.

For the Christian education of children, for the guidance of youth, and for the spiritual well-being of adults:
We offer you ourselves, our time and talents and income.

For the Christian character of our city, and for a spirit of tolerance and good will:
We offer you ourselves, our time and talents and income.

For the calling of the world to Christ, and for the economic and spiritual elevation of untold millions:

We offer you ourselves, our time and talents and income.

For the sake of that day when the spirit of Christ shall clothe itself in the hearts of our age, and swords shall be beaten into plowshares, and peace shall embrace the world:
We offer you ourselves, our time and talents and income.

Let us pray.

Silence

Almighty and everlasting God, you have given us new life in Christ, and Christian homes, and a Christian land: accept the gifts which symbolize the giving of our lives to you. Transform the money we give into programs which enlarge our vision and strengthen your Church. In Jesus' name we pray. *Amen.*

Leader and People

> *We give Thee but Thine own*
> *Whate'er the gift may be;*
> *All that we have is Thine alone,*
> *A trust, O Lord, from Thee. Amen.*

CHARLES F. JACOBS
–WORSHIP SERVICES FOR SPECIAL OCCASIONS

164

Prayer and the Church

Its Unity

•115 The Week of Prayer for Christian Unity

We are come together in the presence of Almighty God to offer him our worship and praise and thanksgiving, to make confession of our sins and to pray for the recovery of the unity of Christ's Church and for the renewal of our common life together, through Jesus Christ in whom we are all made one.

An Act of Penitence

Let us first ask God's forgiveness for the sins by which we have hindered the recovery of unity and caused the Christian name to be blasphemed.
Lord, have mercy upon us.
Christ, have mercy upon us.

For the sins of thought; for ignornace of the faith by which our fellow Christians live; for intellectual pride and isolation; and for the rejection of truth which we have never tried to understand.
Lord, have mercy upon us.
Christ, have mercy upon us.

For the sins of temper; for apathy and complacency, for prejudice and party spirit; for hasty judgment and embittred controversy.
Lord, have mercy upon us.
Christ, have mercy upon us.

Pardon, O Lord, we pray you, the sins of our past ignorance and willfulness; uplift our hearts in love and energy and devotion, that, being made clean from guilt and shame, we may go forward to serve you and your Church in newness of life, through Jesus Christ our Lord. *Amen.*

An Act of Dedication

Let us now give heed to the words of Holy Scripture setting forth God's will and purpose for the unity of his Church.

"Hear, O Israel, the Lord our God is one Lord; and you shall love the Lord your God with all yur heart, and with all your soul, and with all your mind."
Lord, write your Word in our Hearts:
That we may know and do your will.

"There is one body, and one Spirit, as there is also one hope held out in God's call to you; one Lord, one faith, one baptism; one God and Father of all, who is over all and through all and in all."
Lord, write your Word in our Hearts:
That we may know and do your will.

"For Christ is like a single body with its many limbs and organs which, many as they are, together make up one body. For indeed we were all brought into one body by baptism, in the one Spirit, whether we are Jews or Greeks, whether slaves or free, and that one Holy Spirit was poured out for all of us to drink."
Lord, write your Word in our Hearts:
That we may know and do your will.

"But it is not for these alone that I pray, but for those also who through their words put their faith in me; may they all be one; as you, Father, are in me, and I in you, so also may they be in us, that the world may believe that you have sent me."
Lord, write your Word in our Hearts:
That we may know and do your will. Amen.

PRAYERS FOR TODAY'S CHURCH*

•116 At an Ecumenical Prayer Service

Let us pray that all God's will for the Church may be fulfilled in it. And on this day let us pray particularly that all ecumenical endeavors might be based firmly upon the Word of God, might have the aim of glorifying the Son of God, might seek the power of the Spirit of God, might bear fruit to the praise of God.
Lord in your mercy:
Hear our prayer.

Let us pray that, in spite of its present divisions, the Church may preach the gospel with growing zeal, growing confidence, and growing power; so may the gospel itself unite us. And let us pray that the unity thus given may itself commend and make persuasive the gospel we proclaim.
Lord, in your mercy:
Hear our prayer.

Let us pray that we may be saved from worshiping any tradition, no matter how excellent. Let us pray that we may be saved from worshiping any hope, no matter how glorious. Let us pray that we may be saved from these and all forms of idolatry and set free to worship God the Father Almighty.
Lord, in your mercy:
Hear our prayer.

Let us pray for all theologians, thinkers and planners who are now engaged in finding the way to outward expressions of unity, that they may deal in godliness and in truth, and exercise their judgment in wisdom and love.
Lord, in your mercy:
Hear our prayer.

Let us pray for all who negotiate any difficult and painful matter which may arise in practical schemes of union, that they may never forget that they are not dealing with institutions, but with people and with the risen Christ.
Lord, in your mercy:
Hear our prayer.

Let us pray for every experiment designed to help us see the other's tradition through the other's eyes.
Lord, in your mercy:
Hear our prayer.

Let us pray for ourselves in our worship together that our eyes may not be upon each other, nor upon our differences, but upon Christ: that we may look to him and be saved.
Lord, in your mercy:
Hear our prayer.

Let us pray for the churches in this community *(here they may be mentioned by name)* that each may be blessed by God the Holy Spirit and be brought to that fullness of life in which we stand together under the Lordship of Christ.
Lord, in your mercy:
Hear our prayer.

Let us pray for the children of our churches that to them may be revealed the unfolding purposes of God's will and the vision of the Church as it shall be.
Lord, in your mercy:
Hear our prayer.

And let us pray for ourselves that we may be given a vision of the world in all its need, and be so inspired by God that we may serve it with grace and power, and so love the truth, and live the truth, and speak the truth that people everywhere may find the truth, and, being set free from sin, enjoy the glorious liberty of the children of God.
Lord, in your mercy:
Hear our prayer.

And may the grace of our Lord Jesus Christ,
and the love of God,
and the fellowship of the Holy Spirit
be with us all evermore. Amen.

PRAYERS FOR TODAY'S CHURCH

•117 Growing Together in Christ

Let us thank God that, because we are all made in his image, it is possible for all to be united. Let us thank God for the special unity which those who are new creatures in Christ Jesus can enjoy. Let us ask God to forgive the sin that has destroyed the unity he intended for humanity.
Lord of mercy:
Hear our prayer.

Let us thank God for the growth of understanding between Christians of different outlooks and traditions. Let us thank God for the growth in unity of our local churches. Let us pray that we may grow together in truth and love.
Lord of mercy:
Hear our prayer.

Let us pray that we may learn from Christians of other traditions. Let us pray that they may learn from us. May they and we remember that Jesus prayed for us to be sanctified in truth before he prayed for us to be one. May God so guide us that we might seek unity through the truth.
Lord of mercy:
Hear our prayer.

Let us pray for our own church, that we an all its members may be filled with the spirit of faith, hope and love, and so attain to that unity which will lead people to acknowledge the truth of the Gospel.
Lord of mercy:
Hear our prayer.

Let us pray for the local community of which we are a part. Let us pray for greater unity between its various sections, interests and age-groups.

Lord of mercy:
Hear our prayer.

Let us pray for the unity of our country, for a greater understanding and sympathy between the young and those who are older, between employers and those they employ, between migrant workers and their host communities, and between the Church and those who have rejected institutional Christianity.
Lord of mercy:
Hear our prayer.

Finally let us pray for the unity of the world, for reconciliation, peace and compassion between rich and poor, white and non-white, capitalist and communist, and those nations which have long been embattled one against the other.
Lord of mercy:
Hear our prayer.

Silence

Lord Jesus Christ, you said to your apostles,
"Peace I give to you;
my own peace I leave with you":
Regard not our sins, but the faith of your Church,
and give to us the peace and unity of that heavenly City,
where with the Father and the Holy Spirit
you live and reign,
now and for ever. Amen.

PRAYERS FOR TODAY'S CHURCH
AND THE BOOK OF COMMON PRAYER 1979

•118 The Ecumenical Church

God has so adjusted the body, that there may be no discord in the body, but that the members may have the same care for one another. If one member suffers, all suffer together; if one member is honored, all rejoice together.

Now you are the body of Christ and individualy members of it. Therefore let us pray:

For the whole Church of Christ, scattered abroad on six continents, and bearing many names, that it may no longer be torn asunder, divided in itself, or weak, but may become a glorious Church, without spot or blemish, fulfilling your perfect will:

Your will be done in your Church, we pray, O Lord.

For the churches that are passing through times of suffering and persecution, that their faith and courage may not fail or their love grow cold:
Save them and us, we pray, O Lord.

For the churches that are strong in faith, that they may abound in grace and in knowledge and love of you:
Use them and us, we pray, O Lord.

For all weak and struggling churches, that they may persevere and be strong, overcoming those forces which hinder their growth or threaten their existence:
Sustain them and us, we pray, O Lord.

For the newer churches of Asia, Africa, and the islands of the sea, that they may grow into the full stature of the completeness of Christ, bringing new treasures into the Church of the ages:
Direct their steps and ours, we pray, O Lord.

For the older churches of the East and the West, that they may increase in wisdom and humility and find new ways to make the message of the gospel understood in the world of today:
Renew them and us, we pray, O Lord.

For our fellowship as Christians, that we may hold fast to the truth, be delivered from all error, and walk with one another in the way of love and unity:
Teach us and guide us, we pray, O Lord.

For the ecumenical councils of churches, that through them Christians may more quickly overcome their reluctance to cooperate with one another, transcend their differences, and be knit together in a fellowship of understanding and love:
Draw all churches nearer to one another, we pray, O Lord.

Silence

O sovereign and almighty God,
bless all people and all your flock.
Give your peace and your love
to us your servants
that we may be united in the bond of peace,
in one body and one spirit,
in one hope of our calling,
in your divine and boundless love,
for the sake of Jesus Christ,
the great Shepherd of the sheep. Amen.

•119 The Various Christian Communions

Let us give thanks to God for the gifts and graces of each branch of the one great family of Christians.

For the Roman Catholic Church: its glorious traditions, its disciplines of holiness, its worship, rich with the religious passion of the centuries; its noble company of martyrs, teachers, and saints:
We thank you, O Lord, and bless your holy name.

For the Eastern Orthodox Church: its secret treasures of mystical experience; its venerable liturgy; its regard for life in community, and its common will as a source of authority:
We thank you, O Lord, and bless your holy name.

For the Congregationalist concern for the rightful independence of the soul and of the group:
We thank you, O Lord, and bless your holy name.

For the Baptist emphasis on personal regeneration and the conscious relation of the mature soul to the Lord:
We thank you, O Lord, and bless your holy name.

For the powerful ability of Methodists to awaken the conscience of Christians to social evils; and for their emphasis upon the witness of experience and the fruits of the disciplined life:
We thank you, O Lord, and bless your holy name.

For the Presbyterian reverence for the sovereignty of God and their confidence in God's faithfulness to his covenant; for their sense of the moral law, expressing itself in constitutional government:
We thank you, O Lord, and bless your holy name.

For the Quaker witness to the perpetual real presence of the inner light in every human soul, and for their faithful continuance of a free prophetic ministry and Christian non-violence:
We thank you, O Lord, and bless your holy name.

For the Lutheran devotion to the grace of God and the Word of God, enshrined in the ministry of the Word and Sacraments:
We thank you, O Lord, and bless your holy name.

For the Anglican Church: its reverent and temperate ways, through its Catholic heritage and its Protestant conscience; its yearning over the divisions of Christendom, and its longing to be used as a house of reconciliation:
We thank you, O Lord, and bless your holy name.

For the numberless Free Churches, many humble and without splendor, in slum or rural isolation, speaking the gospel to those unwelcome or uninspired in other congregations:
We thank you, O Lord, and bless your holy name.

O God, grant to all these families within your one great Church that, as they come from east and west and north and south to sit down in your kingdom, each may lay at your feet that special grace and gift with which you have endowed it; in Christ's name we pray. *Amen.*

THE STUDENT PRAYER BOOK*

•120 Affirmations and Thanksgivings For Use at Ecumenical Gatherings

The Leader says:

We are the people of God,
and we are one in Christ.
We are one in Christ.

We are in a new age,
and our unity is made more clear,
an indication of our Lord's intention
that all be one in him.
We are one in Christ.

Challenged by our world,
and alive within it,
we rejoice to discover our common concerns,
and are heartened by our common devotion.
We are one in Christ.

Yet it is not that our oneness comes only as we renounce our inheritance.
It is rather that we come, as the Magi,
each with our gift to the Lord
whose body is the Church,
each with our saints.

One of the Reformed tradition says:

We give Calvin, and Knox, and Wesley.
We give order, and simplicity, and justice.
And we are grateful for the gift.

One of Anglican tradition says:

We give Cranmer, and Hooker, and Temple.
We give liturgy, and moderation, and social concern.
And we are grateful for the gift.

One of the Baptist tradition says:

We give Williams, and Moody, and Graham.
We give emotion, and fervor, and freedom.
And we are grateful for the gift.

One of the Lutheran tradition says:

We give Luther, and Bach, and Bonhoeffer.
We give theology, and music, and piety.
And we are grateful for the gift.

One of the Roman Catholic tradition says:

We give Augustine, and Aquinas, and John XXIII.
We give structure, and heritage, and renewal.
And we are grateful for the gift.

One of the Orthodox tradition says:

We give Chrysostom, and Basil, and Berdyaev.
We give continuity, and mystical vision, and life in community.
And we are grateful for the gift.

The Leader says:

We come with these gifts,
with our talents and our vocations,
as we are in the Lord.
And as we are, now, we pray.
For this, our oneness in Christ:
Lord, we thank you.

For the hope of the city of God:
Lord, we thank you.

For the determination to be found
as free men and women before you:
Lord, we thank you.

For faith that trusts in you alone:
Lord, we thank you.

For the continuing renewal of your church:
Lord, we thank you.

For all the kinds of Christians,
we are grateful,
acknowledging the Spirit's work in our distinctions,
and praying for the grace to perceive
the divisiveness that pride creates.
In that we are separated sisters and brothers
by reason of our own fault,
perpetuating the sins of the centuries:
Forgive us, dear Lord,
and unite us in your love.
Amen.

CARL T. UEHLING

• 121 One with the Trinity in Unity

God the Father,
God the Son,
God the Holy Spirit,
Blessed One in Three:
Grant us unity.

Lord, that we may not be afraid
To make friends with strangers,
And accept the different with an open mind:
Grant us faith.

Lord, that we may know each man,
Each woman, each child
To be with us joint heirs through Christ
To all eternity:
Grant us love.

Lord, that we may live the witness
Of your desire,
Not ours:
Grant us obedience.

Lord, that we may build One Church

Of your creation,
Not ours:
Grant us humility.
Amen.

KAY SMALLZRIED

•122 An Act of Dedication

The members of the community face one another across the center aisle or stand in a large circle around the altar or the font, with two leaders saying,

1: Let us make a common act of dedication.

> *Silence*

> In the first century, Paul said to the Church at Rome:
> "All of us, in union with Christ, form one body, and as parts of it we belong to each other.

2: "The life and death of each of us has its influence on others; if we live, we live for the Lord; and if we die, we die for the Lord, so that alive or dead we belong to the Lord."
    We hear your truth, Lord. Help us to do it.

1: In the first century, Paul said to the Church at Corinth:
    "Now together you are Christ's body; but each of you a different part of it.

2: "If one part is hurt, all parts are hurt with it. If one part is given special honor, all parts enjoy it."
    We hear your truth, Lord. Help us to do it.

1: In the first century, Paul said to the Church in Galatia:
    "My brothers and sisters, serve one another in works of love.

2: "If you go snapping at each other and tearing each other to pieces, you had better watch out or you will destroy the whole community."
    We hear your truth, Lord. Help us to do it.

1: In the first letter of John, it is said:
    "We have passed out of death and into life. Of this we can be sure, because we love our brothers and sisters in Christ.

2: "Our love is not to be just words or mere talk, but something real and active; only by this can we be certain that we are children of the truth."
    We hear your truth, Lord. Help us to do it.

1: In this century, Dietrich Bonhoeffer has said:
"It is grace, nothing but grace, that we are allowed to live in community with fellow Christians.

2: "We belong to one another only through and in Jesus Christ."
We hear your truth, Lord. Help us to do it.

1: Jesus said, "You must love the Lord your God with all your heart, and with all your soul, and with all your mind, and with all your strength.

2: "And you must love your neighbor as yourself."
We hear your truth, Lord. Help us to do it. Amen.

HORACE ALLEN

Its Sacraments

•123 Enrolling Candidates for Baptism

The Candidates stand together at the front of the church while the person appointed leads the litany.

In peace let us pray to the Lord, saying "Lord, have mercy."

For these catechumens, that they may remember this day on which they were chosen for Baptism, and remain ever grateful for this heavenly blessing, let us pray to the Lord.
Lord, have mercy.

That they may use this [Lenten] season wisely, joining with us in acts of self-denial and in performing works of mercy, let us pray to the Lord.
Lord, have mercy.

For their teachers, that they may make known to those whom they teach the riches of the Word of God, let us pray to the Lord.
Lord, have mercy.

For their sponsors, that in their private lives and public actions they may show to these candidates a pattern of life in accordance with the Gospel, let us pray to the Lord.
Lord, have mercy.

For their families and friends, that they may place no obstacles in the way of these candidates, but rather assist them to follow the promptings of the Spirit, let us pray to the Lord.
Lord, have mercy.

For this congregation, that [during this Lenten season] it may abound in love and persevere in prayer, let us pray to the Lord.

Lord, have mercy.

For our Bishop, and for all the clergy and people, let us pray to the Lord.
Lord, have mercy.

For all who have died in the hope of the resurrection, and for all the departed, let us pray to the Lord.
Lord, have mercy.

In the communion of [_____ and of all the] saints, let us commend ourselves, and one another, and all our life, to Christ our God.
To you, O Lord our God.

Silence

The Presiding Minister says the following prayer with hands extended over the candidates:

Immortal God, Lord Jesus Christ, the protector of all who come to you, the life of those who believe, and the resurrection of the dead: We call upon you for these your servants who desire the grace of spiritual rebirth in the Sacrament of Holy Baptism. Accept them, Lord Christ, as you promised when you said, "Ask, and it will be given you; seek, and you will find; knock, and it will be opened to you." Give now, we pray, to those who ask, let those who seek find, open the gate to those who knock; that these your servants may receive the everlasting benediction of your heavenly washing, and come to that promised kingdom which you have prepared, and where you live and reign for ever and ever. *Amen.*

THE BOOK OF OCCASIONAL SERVICES

•124 For Catechumens Preparing for Baptism

Let us now pray for *these persons* who *are* to receive the Sacrament of new birth.

Deliver *them*, O Lord, from the way of sin and death.
Lord, hear our prayer.

Open *their* hearts to your grace and truth.
Lord, hear our prayer.

Fill *them* with your holy and life-giving Spirit.
Lord, hear our prayer.

Keep *them* in the faith and communion of your holy Church.

Lord, hear our prayer.

Teach *them* to love others in the power of the Spirit.
Lord, hear our prayer.

Send *them* into the world in witness to your love.
Lord, hear our prayer.

Bring *them* to the fullness of your peace and glory.
Lord, hear our prayer.

Grant, O Lord, that all who are baptized into the death of Jesus Christ your Son may live in the power of his resurrection and look for him to come again in glory; who lives and reigns now and for ever. *Amen.*

THE BOOK OF COMMON PRAYER 1979

•125 For Those To Be Baptized

Lord Jesus Christ, you desire that everyone who follows you shall be born again by water and the Spirit: Remember your servants who *tomorrow* are to be baptized in your Name.

By their names, Lord:
Grant that you will know them, and call them to a life of service.

By their names, Lord:
Grant that they may become the persons you created them to be.

By their names, Lord:
Grant that they may be written for ever in your Book of Life.

Through the water of their baptism, Lord:
Grant that they may be united with you in your death.

Through the water of their baptism, Lord:
Grant that they may receive forgiveness for all their sins.

Through the water of their baptism, Lord:
Grant that they may have power to endure, and strength to have victory in the battle of life.

As members of your Church, Lord:
Grant that they may rise to a new life in the fellowship of those who love you.

As members of your Church, Lord:

Grant that they may suffer when another suffers, and when another rejoices, rejoice.

As members of your Church, Lord:
Grant that they may be your faithful soldiers and servants until their life's end.

Through the abiding presence of your Spirit, Lord:
Grant that they may lead the rest of their lives according to this beginning.

Through the abiding presence of your Spirit, Lord:
Grant that when they pass through the dark waters of death, you will be with them.

Through the abiding presence of your Spirit, Lord:
Grant that they may inherit the kingdom of glory prepared for them from the foundation of the world.

To you, Lord Christ, with the Father and the Holy Spirit, be honor and glory in the Church, now and for ever. Amen.

THE BOOK OF OCCASIONAL SERVICES

•126 At the Baptism of an Infant or Young Child

Lord, you want little children to come to you, grant that this child may show us the way.

As this child is helpless without us,
may we learn how helpless we are without God.
Lord, in your mercy:
Hear our prayer.

As this child is curious to explore the world,
may we be curious to explore the ways of faith.
Lord, in your mercy:
Hear our prayer.

As this child will trust and be open to us,
may we learn to trust God's ways for us.
Lord, in your mercy:
Hear our prayer.

As this child cries until *his* physical needs are satisfied,
may we cry out to the living God until our spiritual needs are satisfied.

Lord, in your mercy:
Hear our prayer.

As this child smiles at all who take an interest in *him,*
may we daily exhibit the joy of those who are loved by God.
Lord, in your mercy:
Hear our prayer.

Lord, we come before you with open hands and empty hearts.
Pour the fullness of your grace into our hands and hearts,
that as children we may seek and find the joys of your Kingdom. Amen.

PRAYERS OF THE FAITHFUL

•127 At the Naming or Dedication of a Newborn Child

Happy the humble in spirit, for theirs is the kingdom of heaven; happy the
gentle, for they shall have the earth as their heritage.
Forgive us, Lord, our arrogant and grasping spirit and our self-sufficient ways;
forgive us the violence we do each day to our neighbors and to the earth which
is our home.

Happy those who mourn, for they shall be comforted; happy those who
hunger and thirst for what is right, for they shall be satisfied.
Forgive us our insensitivity to the pain and sorrow around us, our indifference
to injustice which others have to endure.

Happy the merciful and the pure in heart; they shall have mercy shown to
them, they shall see God.
Show us mercy and forgive us, Lord, though we are unwilling to forgive; clean
away the dirt in our lives that we may more clearly mirror your goodness.

Happy the peacemakers and those who are persecuted in the cause of right;
they shall be God's children, they shall share in God's kingdom.
Help us love peace, practice it and suffer for it; and though we have failed,
renew us, Lord, in our yearning for your kingdom.

You are the salt of the earth.
Give us greater faith that may add flavor to every thing we do.

You are the light of the world.
Give us greater hope that may restore purpose to every life we touch.

You are the lamp on the lamp-stand.

Give us greater love that may bring joy to every one we meet.

As _____ shines today as a light newly lit in our lives, giving us new cause
for faith and hope and love,
*So let us shine as lights in the midst of the world that, seeing our good works
and knowing their source, those around us may give praise and glory to our
heavenly Father. Amen.*

JEFFERY W. ROWTHORN

•128 The Renewal of Baptismal Vows

Through the Paschal mystery, dear friends, we are buried with Christ by
Baptism into his death, and raised with him to newness of life. I call upon
you, therefore, to renew the solemn promises and vows of Holy Baptism, by
which we once renounced Satan and all his works, and promised to serve
God faithfully in his holy catholic Church.

Do you reaffirm your renunciation of evil and renew your commitment to
Jesus Christ?
I do.

Do you believe in God the Father?
I believe in God, the Father almighty, creator of heaven and earth.

Do you believe in Jesus Christ, the Son of God?
I believe in Jesus Christ, his only Son, our Lord.
He was conceived by the power of the Holy Spirit
  and born of the Virgin Mary.
He suffered under Pontius Pilate, was crucified, died, and was buried.
He descended to the dead.
On the third day he rose again.
He ascended into heaven, and is seated at the right hand of the Father.
He will come again to judge the living and the dead.

Do you believe in God the Holy Spirit?
I believe in the Holy Spirit, the holy catholic Church,
the communion of saints, the forgiveness of sins,
the resurrection of the body, and the life everlasting.

Will you continue in the apostles' teaching and fellowship, in the breaking of
bread, and in the prayers?
I will, with God's help.

Will you persevere in resisting evil and, whenever you fall into sin, repent
and return to the Lord?

I will, with God's help.

Will you proclaim by word and example the Good News of God in Christ?
I will, with God's help.

Will you seek and serve Christ in all persons, loving your neighbor as yourself?
I will, with God's help.

Will you strive for justice and peace among all people, and respect the dignity of every human being?
I will, with God's help.

The Celebrant concludes the Renewal of Baptismal Vows with these words:

May Almighty God, the Father of our Lord Jesus Christ, who has given us a new birth by water and the Holy Spirit, and bestowed upon us the forgiveness of sins, keep us in eternal life by his grace, in Christ Jesus our Lord. *Amen.*

THE BOOK OF COMMON PRAYER 1979*

• 129 In Thanksgiving for Baptism

In baptism, we die with Christ and rise with him to a new life. St. Paul explains the meaning of our baptism in the letter to the Romans. "Do you not know that all of us who have been baptized into Christ Jesus were baptized into his death? We were buried therefore with him by baptism into death, so that as Christ was raised from the dead by the glory of the Father, we too might walk in newness of life. For if we have been united with him in a death like his, we shall certainly be united with him in a resurrection like his. We know that our old self was crucified with him so that the sinful body might be destroyed, and we might no longer be enslaved to sin. For those who have died are freed from sin. But if we have died with Christ, we believe that we shall also live with him. For we know that Christ being raised from the dead will never die again; death no longer has dominion over him. The death he died he died to sin, once for all, but the life he lives he lives to God. So you also must consider yourselves dead to sin and alive to God in Christ Jesus." (Romans 6:3–11)

Let us pray, giving thanks to the Lord for the gift of baptism which we have all received.

Silent prayer

Christ is our life!

We praise you, O Lord, and we thank you.

For the gift of dying with Christ:
We praise you, O Lord, and we thank you.

For the gift of rising in victory with Christ:
We praise you, O Lord, and we thank you.

For the gift of our new life in Christ:
We praise you, O Lord, and we thank you.

For the gift of adoption by our heavenly Father:
We praise you, O Lord, and we thank you.

For the gift of membership in Christ's mystical Body, the Church:
We praise you, O Lord, and we thank you.

For the gift of the common priesthood we all share with Christ our High Priest:
We praise you, O Lord, and we thank you.

For the gift of joining with Christ to offer ourselves as a living sacrifice to the Father:
We praise you, O Lord, and we thank you.

For the gift of our whole sacramental life, which starts with baptism:
We praise you, O Lord, and we thank you.

For the gift of the Holy Spirit, who dwells in our midst.
We praise you, O Lord, and we thank you.

For these and all the gifts and graces of baptism:
We praise you, O Lord, and we thank you.

SCRIPTURE SERVICES

•130 Baptism in the Spirit

Lord and life-giving Spirit, who brooded over the waters when first the world began:
Make us dead to sin but alive to God.

Who led your people out of slavery through the waters of the Red Sea and into freedom through the waters of the Jordan:
Make us dead to sin but alive to God.

Who overshadowed Mary of Nazareth and caused her to be the mother of God's only Son:

Make us dead to sin but alive to God.

Who anointed Jesus as Messiah as he was baptized by John in the Jordan:
Make us dead to sin but alive to God.

Who raised Jesus from the grave and proclaimed him Son of God in all his power:
Make us dead to sin but alive to God.

Who appeared in tongues of flame on Pentecost:
Make us dead to sin but alive to God.

Who charges the waters of baptism through and through with power to give new life:
Make us dead to sin but alive to God.

Lord, hear our prayer:
Let our cry come to you.

Let us pray:

Almighty and everlasting God, who out of pure mercy decreed both the creation and the renewal of the world, be present and active in the sacraments which you have instituted for our salvation. Send forth the Spirit of adoption in full measure that those who are born of water and the Spirit may live under the power of that same Spirit all the days of their life and so arrive safely in their heavenly home; through Jesus Christ our Lord. *Amen.*

PRAY LIKE THIS

• 131 Offertory Prayers

These prayers may be used as the offering of money is presented and the Bread and Wine placed on the Table and made ready.

At the presentation of the money-offering

Blessed are you, Lord, God of all creation.
Through your goodness we have this money to offer, the fruit of our labor and of the skills you have given us.

Take us and our possessions to do your work in the world.
Blessed be God for ever.

At the presentation of the Bread

Blessed are you, Lord, God of all creation.

Through your goodness we have this bread to offer, which earth has given and human hands have made.

It will become for us the bread of life.
Blessed be God for ever.

At the presentation of the Wine

Blessed are you, Lord, God of all creation.
Through your goodness we have this wine to offer, fruit of the vine and work of human hands.

It will become our spiritual drink.
Blessed be God for ever.

THE ANGLICAN CHURCH OF THE PROVINCE OF SOUTH AFRICA
AND THE ENGLISH TRANSLATION OF THE ROMAN MISSAL, 1973*

•132 Give Us This Day Our Daily Bread
– A Communion Litany –

Let us pray, asking the Lord for the grace of sharing in the heavenly meal with him.

Silence

Come, eat of my food, and drink of the wine I have mixed!
Give us this day our daily bread.

Blessed are all who shall feast in the kingdom of God.
Give us this day our daily bread.

The kingdom of heaven is like a king who made a marriage feast for his son.
Give us this day our daily bread.

I appoint to you a kingdom, even as my Father has appointed to me, that you may eat and drink at my table in my kingdom.
Give us this day our daily bread.

I tell you that many will come from the east and from the west, from the north and from the south, and will feast with Abraham, Isaac, and Jacob in the kingdom of heaven.
Give us this day our daily bread.

Jesus took the five loaves and the two fishes and, looking up to heaven, blessed and broke the loaves, and gave them to the disciples to set before the people.

Give us this day our daily bread.

Take and eat; this is my body.
Give us this day our daily bread.

All of you drink of this; for this is my blood of the new covenant, which is being shed for many unto the forgiveness of sins.
Give us this day our daily bread.

But I say to you, I will not drink henceforth of this fruit of the vine, until that day when I shall drink it new with you in the kingdom of my Father.
Give us this day our daily bread. Amen.

SCRIPTURE SERVICES

•133 The Sacrament of Unity
– A Communion Litany –

Let us pray, giving thanks to the Lord who bestows on us the great mystery of his love in this Eucharistic meal.

Silence

Because the bread is one, we, though many, are one body, all of us who partake of the one bread.
We are one in his body and one in his love.

This is my body which shall be given up for you; do this in remembrance of me.
We are one in his body and one in his love.

A new commandment I give you, that you love one another; that as I have loved you, you also love one another.
We are one in his body and one in his love.

As the Father has loved me, I also have loved you. Abide in my love.
We are one in his body and one in his love.

Do not labor for the food that perishes, but for that which endures to life everlasting, which the Son of Man will give you.
We are one in his body and one in his love.

I am the bread of life. All who come to me shall not hunger, and all who believe in me shall never thirst.
We are one in his body and one in his love.

Now you are the body of Christ, and each of you individually a member of it.
We are one in his body and one in his love. Amen.

SCRIPTURE SERVICES

•134 Litany at the Breaking of the Bread

Lamb of God,
you take away the sins of the world,
have mercy on us.
Lamb of God,
you take away the sins of the world,
have mercy on us.

Is not the cup of blessing we bless
a sharing in the blood of Christ?
Is not the bread we break
a sharing in the body of Christ?
Lamb of God, have mercy on us.

Because the loaf of bread is one bread,
many though we are,
we are one body, the body of Christ.
Lamb of God, have mercy on us.

Living bread from Heaven,
feed us now and evermore.
Lamb of God, have mercy on us.

Whoever eats this bread will live forever!
Lamb of God, have mercy on us.

Lamb of God,
you take away the sins of the world,
grant us peace.
Lamb of God,
you take away the sins of the world,
grant us peace. Amen.

THE LITURGICAL COMMISSION OF THE DIOCESE OF BROOKLYN*

• 135 An Early English Post-Communion Litany

The response to each line is: "Christ within me, I adore Thee."

Welcome, my gracious Creator! *Response.*
Welcome, my kindly Redeemer and Savior!
Welcome, thou high rich King and worthy Prince!
Welcome, my sweet love!
Welcome, my kindly Father!
Welcome, my tender Nurse and Mother!
Welcome, my Brother!
Welcome, my Helper and Teacher!
Welcome, my castle and tower, my safe refuge and protection!
Welcome, my very God that died on the rood!
Welcome, my sweet Jesu, that for me sheddest thy heart-blood!
Welcome, Son of the Virgin Mary!
Welcome, my Lord of great mercy and rightful Judge when I shall die!
Welcome, thou very joy and food of angels!
Welcome, thou love and happiness of all the saints!
Welcome, thou desire and comfort of all Christian souls!
Welcome, my very hope and health!
Welcome, all my felicity, solace, comfort, and my endless wealth!

Good Lord, grant me for to feel thy presence ghostly and inwardly; array me with thy gracious virtues, and inflame me with thy holy love, and give me them all: for then have I all that I covet, and all that I desire, and all that I need.
Christ within me, I adore Thee. Amen.

KYRIE ELEISON*

• 136 A Thanksgiving for the Bread of Life

Be praised, Lord,
by parents
who set on the table each day
the fruit of their work:
bread of a life of contentment,
bread of a life full of difficulties,
so that their children might grow to adulthood.

Praise and glory be yours, for ever.

Be praised, Lord,
by the poor who each morning
must beg again for
the bread of tears and misery
and who sometimes taste human compassion
in a loaf offered to them and shared.
Praise and glory be yours, for ever.

Be praised, Lord,
by the radical reformers of society
who offer heart and life
so that their poor brothers and sisters
might one day taste abundantly
the bread earned by their own sweat.
Praise and glory be yours, for ever.

Be praised, Lord,
by engineers and technicians
serving in poor nations
so that a more productive and well-tended earth
might yield a plentiful harvest of wheat and rice and beans.
Praise and glory be yours, for ever.

Be praised, Lord,
for your presence
alongside parents of families,
alongside beggars, engineers and reformers.
Your presence is mysterious and difficult to grasp,
and yet so strong and real
that we can derive life from it,
just as we live by eating bread.
Praise and glory be yours, for ever.

Be praised, Lord,
by your Son, Jesus Christ,
in a way surpassed by no other.
He multiplied bread for the poor
and took his place at table with sinners.
Then on the night before his passion,
at that moment, in order to become the least among us all,
he became bread pulled apart and broken,
passed from hand to hand and shared.
Praise and glory be yours, for ever. Amen.

PRAYERS IN COMMUNITY

Ministry

•137 A Litany of Election

Blessed be the God and Father of our Lord Jesus Christ who chose us before the foundation of the world!
Blessed be our God and Father!

God has chosen us to be holy and without blemish in union with the Son.
Blessed be our God and Father!

We were chosen in the Son who is the Head of the Church.
We are one with the Son for we are members of his Body.
Blessed be our God and Father!

God has chosen some as apostles, some as prophets, some to one task, others to another. God calls all of us to a work of ministry in the Body of the Son.
We will choose what God has chosen.

God has chosen some to be bishops and priests in the Church.
We will choose what God has chosen.

God has chosen some to be husbands and wives, some to be monks and religious in the Church.
We will choose what God has chosen.

God has chosen some to study and some to work with their hands for the building up of the Body of Christ.
We will choose what God has chosen.

But all these things are the work of one and the same Spirit, who calls everyone according to God's will.
We will choose what God has chosen.

Blessed be the God and Father of our Lord Jesus Christ who has called us to life in the Church! God has chosen us to be sons and daughters in his Son. *We will choose what God has chosen. We will live as God's sons and daughters in the Church. Amen.*

SCRIPTURE SERVICES

• 138 Our Ministry as Servants

This may be led by two voices.

> *The Lord calls us to be servants. Let us rejoice!*

1: Be generous and share your food with the poor. You will be blessed for it. (Proverbs 22:9)
> *The Lord calls us to be servants. Let us rejoice!*

2: If you oppress poor people, you insult the God who made them; but kindness shown to the poor is an act of worship. (Proverbs 14:31)
> *The Lord calls us to be servants. Let us rejoice!*

1: Defend the rights of the poor and the orphans; be fair to the needy and the helpless. (Psalm 82:3)
> *The Lord calls us to be servants. Let us rejoice!*

2: A good person knows the rights of the poor, but wicked people cannot understand such things. (Proverbs 29:7)
> *The Lord calls us to be servants. Let us rejoice!*

1: Treat foreigners as you would your own, and love them as you love yourselves. (Leviticus 19:34a)
> *The Lord calls us to be servants. Let us rejoice!*

2: Do not follow the majority when they do wrong, or when they give testimony that perverts justice. (Exodus 23:2)
> *The Lord calls us to be servants. Let us rejoice!*

1: Speak up for people who cannot speak for themselves. Protect the rights of all who are helpless. (Proverbs 31:8)
> *The Lord calls us to be servants. Let us rejoice!*

2: Speak for them and be a righteous judge. Protect the rights of the poor and needy. (Proverbs 31:9)
> *The Lord calls us to be servants. Let us rejoice!*

Silence

Lord, help us love you with all our heart, soul, strength, and mind, and our neighbors as ourselves. We rejoice that we are able to love, because you first loved us; through Christ our Lord. Amen.

BREAD FOR THE WORLD

•139 Your Will Be Done

Let us pray to the Father, asking for grace to drink the cup which God offers us.

Silence for personal prayer

With Christ our Brother we hear the call. With him we answer:
Father, your will be done!
Father, your will be done in us!

Make us strong with the faith of our father Abraham.
Father, your will be done in us!

Make us bold with the courage of Moses, the leader of your people.
Father, your will be done in us!

Enlighten us with the wisdom of Samuel, ruler and judge over Israel.
Father, your will be done in us!

Give us the spirit of discernment and decision so that we may work in your service with the authority of the great king David.
Father, your will be done in us!

Make us alive, as you did Isaiah the prophet, with a sense of your holy presence.
Father, your will be done in us!

Give us, as you gave to John the Baptist, a love of poverty and self-effacement in our labors for the spread of your kingdom.
Father, your will be done in us!

Make us great-hearted, like Paul, so that we may be all things to all people, in Christ Jesus.
Father, your will be done in us!

Shape us, transform us, even as you made the Virgin Mary a perfect instrument in your hands.
Father, your will be done in us!

Let us pray, giving thanks to the Lord for having chosen us for a special role and vocation in the Church.

Silence for personal prayer

O Lord our God, you have chosen us from before the foundation of the world and blessed us with every spiritual blessing. Grant, we pray you, that having been made new through the mystery of our redemption, we may respond fully to the gift of our holy election and restore all people, all things, and ourselves to you; through Christ our Lord. *Amen.*
Lord, what wilt thou have me do?

You have not chosen me, but I have chosen you, and have appointed you that you should go and bear fruit, and that your fruit should remain.
Thanks be to God! Amen.

SCRIPTURE SERVICES

•140 A Litany of the Apostles

Lord Jesus, we remember before you those you called to be your disciples and trained to become your apostles.
They were all of them laypeople, Lord, but you chose them for the extension of your ministry as prophet, priest, and king.

We remember Peter, that strange, uncouth rock made of such shifting sand.
Help us, O Lord, like Peter, to find in you the Christ, the Son of the living God.

We remember Andrew, evangelist extraordinary, who was always bringing someone to you.
Unlock our lips, O Lord, that, like Andrew, we may learn to talk about you with skill and grace.

We remember James and John, "Sons of Thunder," willing vehicles of a mother's ambition.
Chasten and refine our ambitions, O Lord, that, like them, we may learn at last to seek only your will.

We remember Philip, slow of wit, big of heart.
Remind us, O Lord, that you place more stock in our hearts than in our wits.

We remember Thomas, the skeptic, who ached because he wanted so badly to believe.
As you did for Thomas, O Lord, convict us of the power and sufficiency of your resurrection.

We remember Matthew, prosperous, despised, an outcast in the midst of his own people.
Let us not forget, O Lord, that with you no human label ever sticks.

We remember James, your brother, perhaps your rival in your family.
Impress upon us, O Lord, the rightful claim of family ties, and yet their insignificance compared with your claim on us.

We remember Simon, the Zealot.
Keep all of our lesser loyalties, O Lord, even our love of country, subordinate to our loyalty to you.

We remember –we barely remember–your obscure disciples, Thaddeus and Bartholomew.
You know why you chose them, Lord, and, like millions of other obscure disciples, they served you well.

And we remember Judas, though we wish we could forget him.
But we dare not forget him, because he is flesh of our flesh and bone of our bone, and because your love reached out and included even him.

Lord, we thank you for the whole company of your apostles, and for your continuing invitation to discipleship. Amen.

MODELS FOR MINISTERS I*

• 141 Thanksgiving for the Ministry of the Laity

Let us thank God for those persons who have responded to Christ's call to serve him in the world.
Lord, we know that you call us to serve our neighbor in love, not only in church, but also in the world in which we live.

For those who minister to the sick as medical personnel, or through hospital visitation and volunteer work:
We give you thanks, O Lord.

For those who help with the education of our children, both salaried staff and volunteer aides:
We give you thanks, O Lord.

For those who are actively involved in the political process of our community, state, and nation:
We give you thanks, O Lord.

For those who work for social justice, fair housing, and equal opportunity for both sexes and all races:
We give you thanks, O Lord.

For those who visit the lonely and the shut-in, and for those who find time to listen to the troubled and distressed:
We give you thanks, O Lord.

For those who serve through Meals on Wheels and for those who offer counsel and support at walk-in centers or anonymously over the phone:
We give you thanks, O Lord.

For those who work to make our community a safe and pleasant place to live – engineers, bakers, contractors, architects, fire and police personnel:
We give you thanks, O Lord.

For those who work with our children and youth through scouting, tutorial programs, athletic groups, and teen centers:
We give you thanks, O Lord.

For those who seek both to glorify you and to help their neighbor through their work:
We give you thanks, O Lord.

For those who serve as homemakers, providing care, nourishment, and a secure haven for families:
We give you thanks, O Lord.

For all those who labor and whose efforts are often unseen and unsung, but who contribute significantly to Christ's ministry in the world:
We give you thanks, O Lord.

We pray for all who labor faithfully day in and day out.
Work through us and help us always to work for you.

Let us thank God for the love we have experienced in Christ Jesus, which motivates and empowers us to serve others in his name.
O Lord, we recall the words of your Son when he said,
"I came not to be served, but to serve."
He saw our needs, and he ministered to us in love.
We thank you for calling us to follow in his footsteps.
We ask you to keep our eyes open to the possibilities around us
and grant us strength and courage, and the willingness
to continue to serve Christ and all those around us.
In Christ's name, we pray. Amen.

MELVIN VOS
–MONDAY'S MINISTRIES

•142 For Theological Seminaries

During the times of silence specific people may be remembered or mentioned aloud by name.

O God of truth, ever beckoning us to loftier understanding and deeper wisdom, we seek your will and implore your grace for all who share the life of divinity schools and seminaries in our day, knowing that unless you build among us, we who teach and learn will labor but in vain.

Silence

For the men and women who teach, that they may together bring fire and vision to a common task, knowing one field yet eager to relate it to all others; just in their academic demands, yet seeing each student as a child of God; fitted to teach not only by great learning but by great faith in humankind and in you, their God:
In them and in us, O God, kindle your saving truth.

Silence

For deans and presidents, trustees and development officers, and all others who point the way for theological education in our day, that their concern be not mainly budgets and buildings and prestige, but men and women freed to know your whole will and roused to serve you in your Church:
In them and in us, O God, kindle your saving truth.

Silence

For janitors and maids, for cooks and keepers of the grounds, for those who prepare our food and wash our dishes, and for the host of other workers and suppliers whose faithfulness ministers to our common life:
In them and in us, O God, kindle your saving truth.

Silence

For parents and givers of scholarships, who send and support theological students, that they may not desire for them more income, or social acceptance, or glory of family or of donor, but look rather for new breadth of intelligence, the spirit made whole, and devoted Christian service in life:
In them and in us, O God, kindle your saving truth.

Silence

For the students themselves, that their confusion may be brief, their perspective constantly enlarged, and their minds and spirits alert to all that chapel and classroom, library and fieldwork assignment can mean in their lives:
In them and in us, O God, kindle your saving truth.

Silence

For every member of the community of learning and of service, that with them we may be aware of your Holy Spirit leading us all into truth, and may grasp here your special intention for all our learning and striving:
In them and in us, O God, kindle your saving truth.

Silence

We know, O heavenly Father,
that a seminary education is but the willing and planning
of many men and women,
each sought by your great love.
Grant that we who would earnestly serve you
may witness in the world to the reality of your gospel
as it is shown forth in Christ Jesus our Lord. Amen.

JOHN OLIVER NELSON
–THE STUDENT PRAYER BOOK

•143 A Thanksgiving for Music and Musicians

O God our Father, we thank you for music and its wondrous power to touch and heal and strengthen; under its spell the closed doors of the human spirit are unlocked and our hearts are moved to respond to you in worship. We praise you for this most precious gift.

Silence

Let everything that lives praise the Lord.
Thanks be to God!

We thank you for all those who, entrusted with this gift, have "composed musical tunes and set forth verses in writing"; living on among us in their works, they have wonderfully enriched our lives and exalted you in the liturgy of your Church. We praise you for all faithful singers of your song.

Silence

Let everything that lives praise the Lord.
Thanks be to God!

We thank you for all who teach in conservatories and schools of sacred music, interpreting music born in the souls of others and bringing gifts to fruition in many generations of students. We praise you for what they, receiving generously from you, have shared generously with others.

Silence

Let everything that lives praise the Lord.
Thanks be to God!

And lastly we thank you for all who day by day enable us to sing your song in many ways and many places, accompanying it on organ and guitar and trumpet, leading it with the beauty of the solo voice, enriching it with new forms of music, patient scholarship and gifted teaching. We praise you for their ministry and gratefully ask your blessing on it this day.

Silence

Let everything that lives praise the Lord.
Thanks be to God! Amen.

JEFFERY ROWTHORN

•144 A Litany for Ordinations

For use at Ordinations or on Ember Days or other appropriate occasions.

God the Father:
Have mercy on us.

God the Son:
Have mercy on us.

God the Holy Spirit:
Have mercy on us.

Holy Trinity, one God:
Have mercy on us.

We pray to you, Lord Christ.
Lord, hear our prayer.

For the holy Church of God, that it may be filled with truth and love, and be found without fault at the Day of your Coming,
we pray to you, O Lord.
Lord, hear our prayer.

For all members of your Church in their vocation and ministry, that they may serve you in a true and godly life,
we pray to you, O Lord.

Lord, hear our prayer.

For ____, our ____, and for all other ministers, that they may be filled with your love, may hunger for truth, and may thirst after righteousness, we pray to you, O Lord.
Lord, hear our prayer.

For ____, chosen to serve as ____ in your Church, we pray to you, O Lord.
Lord, hear our prayer.

That *he* may faithfully fulfill the duties of this ministry, build up your Church, and glorify your Name, we pray to you, O Lord.
Lord, hear our prayer.

That by the indwelling of the Holy Spirit *he* may be sustained and encouraged to persevere to the end, we pray to you, O Lord.
Lord, hear our prayer.

For *his* family [*or* the members of *his* household *or* comunity], that they may be adorned with all Christian virtues, we pray to you, O Lord.
Lord, hear our prayer.

For all who fear God and believe in you, Lord Christ, that our divisions may cease and that all may be one as you and the Father are one, we pray to you, O Lord.
Lord, hear our prayer.

For the mission of the Church, that in faithfull witness it may preach the Gospel to the ends of the earth, we pray to you, O Lord.
Lord, hear our prayer.

For those who do not yet believe, and for those who have lost their faith, that they may receive the light of the Gospel, we pray to you, O Lord.
Lord, hear our prayer.

For the peace of the world, that a spirit of respect and forebearance may grow among nations and peoples, we pray to you, O Lord.
Lord, hear our prayer.

For those in positions of public trust, especially ____, that they may serve justice and promote the dignty and freedom of every person, we pray to you, O Lord.

Lord, hear our prayer.

For a blessing upon all human labor, and for the right use of the riches of creation, that the world may be freed from poverty, famine, and disaster, we pray to you, O Lord.
Lord, hear our prayer.

For the poor, the persecuted, the sick, and all who suffer; for refugees, prisoners, and all who are in danger; that they may be relieved and protected, we pray to you, O Lord.
Lord, hear our prayer.

For ourselves; for the forgiveness of our sins, and for the grace of the Holy Spirit to amend our lives, we pray to you, O Lord.
Lord, hear our prayer.

For all who have died in the communion of your Church, and those whose faith is known to you alone, that, with all the saints, they may have rest in that place where there is no pain or grief, but life eternal, we pray to you, O Lord.
Lord, hear our prayer.

Rejoicing in the fellowship of the ever-blessed Virgin Mary, *blessed* _____, and all the saints, let us commend ourselves, and one another, and all our life to Christ our God.
To you, O Lord our God.

Lord, have mercy.
Christ, have mercy.
Lord, have mercy.

The Leader concludes with a suitable Collect and the People respond "Amen."

THE BOOK OF COMMON PRAYER 1979

•145 At an Ordination

Leader

We celebrate _____'s ordination as one of Christ's ministers. In doing so, let us remember the mercy of God, and God's call to ministry.

Silence

"Therefore, my brothers and sisters, I implore you by the mercy of God to offer your very selves:

202

*"A living sacrifice, dedicated and fit for God's acceptance, the worship offered
by mind and heart."*

Leader

We celebrate _____'s gifts and skills. In doing so, let us remember the power
of God, and _____'s ministry to us.

Silence

Ordinand

"I was with you in weakness and in much fear and trembling; my speech
and my message did not sway you with subtle arguments, but carried
conviction by spiritual power.
*"So that your faith might be built not upon human wisdom but upon the power
of God."*

Leader

We celebrate _____'s humanity and need of support. In doing so, let us
remember the law of Christ, and our ministry to _____.

Silence

*"If one of you should do something wrong, you who are endowed with the Spirit
must set that person right again very gently. Look to yourself, each one of you,
for you may be tempted, too.*

Ordinand

"And bear one another's burdens, for in this way you will fulfill the law of
Christ."

Leader

We celebrate _____'s readiness to give and to receive. In doing so, let us
remember the gift of the Spirit, and our ministry to one another.

Silence

Ordinand

"Another, by the one Spirit, is granted faith; another, by the same Spirit, the
ability to heal; another the power to do great deeds.
"Each one of us is given the gift of the Spirit to be used to the common good."

Leader

We celebrate _____'s special gifts *(mention may be made here of specific
talents and skills)*. In doing so, let us remember the grace of God, and our
ministry with God in the world.

Silence

"Sharing in God's work, we urge this appeal upon you: you have received the grace of God; do not let it go for nothing.

Ordinand

"We put no obstacle in anyone's way that no fault may be found with our ministry. As God's servants we try to commend ourselves in every circumstance."

Leader

We celebrate our unity with _____ in a common ministry. In doing so, we remember the promise of God, and God's ministry to us.

Silence

"Therefore, my sisters and brothers, stand firm and immovable, and work for the Lord always, since you know that in the Lord your labor is not vain. *"May the grace of our Lord Jesus Christ, and the love of God, and the fellowship of the Holy Spirit be with us all evermore. Amen."*

JEFFERY W. ROWTHORN

• 146 Veni Creator

Come, Holy Ghost, our souls inspire:
And lighten with celestial fire.

Thou the anointing Spirit art:
Who dost thy sev'nfold gifts impart.

Thy blessed unction from above:
Is comfort, life, and fire of love.

Enable with perpetual light:
The dullness of our blinded sight.

Anoint and cheer our soiled face:
With the abundance of thy grace.

Keep far our foes, give peace at home:
Where thou art guide, no ill can come.

Teach us to know the Father, Son:
And thee, of both, to be but One,

That through the ages all along:

This may be our endless song:

Praise to thy eternal merit,
Father, Son, and Holy Spirit. Amen.

LATIN, 9TH CENTURY
– TRANSLATED BY JOHN COSIN*

• 147 For a New Ministry

Representatives of the congregation and of the clergy of the diocese stand before the bishop with the new minister. Any of the presentations that follow may be added to, omitted, or adapted, as appropriate to the nature of the new ministry, and to the order of the minister. In the absence of the bishop, the deputy substitutes the words given in parentheses.

Representatives of the congregation present a Bible, saying:

_____, accept this Bible, and be among us (*or* be in this place) as one who proclaims the Word.
Amen. And may the Lord be with you.

The Bishop presents a vessel of water, saying:

_____, take this water, and help me (help the Bishop) baptize in obedience to our Lord.

Amen. And may the Lord be with you.

Others present a stole or other symbol, saying:

_____, receive this *stole,* and be among us as a pastor and priest.
Amen. And may the Lord be with you.

Others present a book of prayers or other symbol, saying:

_____, receive this *book,* and be among us as a *man* of prayer.
Amen. And may the Lord be with you.

Others present olive oil or some other symbol, saying:

_____, use this *oil,* and be among us as a healer and reconciler.
Amen. And may the Lord be with you.

If the new minister is the rector or vicar of the parish, a Warden may now present the keys of the church, saying:

_____, receive these keys, and let the doors of this place be open to all people.
Amen. And may the Lord be with you.

Representative clergy of the diocese present the Constitution and Canons of this Church, saying:

_____, obey these Canons, and be among us to share in the councils of this diocese.
Amen. And may the Lord be with you.

Other Representatives of the congregation present bread and wine, saying,

_____, take this bread and wine, and be among us to break the Bread and bless the Cup.
Amen. And may the Lord be with you.

The Bishop then says:

_____, let all these be signs of the ministry which is mine and yours (the Bishop's and yours) in this place.
Amen. And may the Lord be with you.

The Bishop then presents the new minister to the congregation, saying:

Greet your new *Rector.*

When appropriate, the family of the new minister may also be presented at this time.

The Congregation expresses its approval. Applause is appropriate.

The Bishop greets the new minister.

The new Minister then says to the people:

The peace of the Lord be always with you.
And also with you.

The new Minister then greets other members of the clergy, family members, and the congregation. The People greet one another.

THE BOOK OF COMMON PRAYER 1979

•148 A Litany for Personal Life (The Southwell Litany)

Originally composed and particularly suitable for retreats and quiet days

Dr. George Ridding, first Bishop of Southwell in England, who composed this Litany for use at meetings of his clergy, was accustomed to introduce it with the following words:

> *Seeing, brethren, that we are weak men but entrusted with a great office, and that we cannot but be liable to hinder the work entrusted to us by our infirmities of body, soul, and spirit, both those common to all men and those specially attaching to our office, let us pray God to save us and help us from the several weaknesses which beset us severally, that he will make us know what faults we have not known, that he will show us the harm of what we have not cared to control, that he will give us strength and wisdom to do more perfectly the work to which our lives have been consecrated – for no less service than the honor of God and the edifying of his Church.*

Lord, open our minds to see ourselves as you see us, or even as others see
 us and we see others;
And from all unwillingness to know our infirmities:
Save us and help us, O Lord.

From moral weakness, from hesitation,
from fear of others and dread of responsibility:
 Strengthen us with courage to speak the truth in love and self-control;
And alike from the weakness of hasty violence
and from the weakness of moral cowardice:
Save us and help us, O Lord.

From weakness of judgment,
from the indecision that can make no choice,
and from the irresolution that carries no choice into act:
 Strengthen our eye to see and our will to choose the right;
And from losing opportunities to serve you,
and from perplexing ourselves and others with uncertainties:
Save us and help us, O Lord.

From infirmity of purpose,
from want of earnest care and interest,
from sluggish indolence and slack indifference,
and from all spiritual deadness of heart:
Save us and help us, O Lord.

From dullness of conscience, from feeble sense of duty,

from thoughtless disregard of consequences to others,
from a low idea of the obligations of our calling,
and from all half-heartedness in our service:
Save us and help us, O Lord.

From weariness in continuing struggles,
from despondency in failure and disappointment,
from overburdened sense of unworthiness,
from morbid fancies of imaginary back-slidings:
    Raise us to a lively hope in your mercy and in the power of faith;
And from all exaggerated fears and vexations:
Save us and help us, O Lord.

From self-conceit, vanity, and boasting,
from delight in supposed success and superiority:
    Raise us to the modesty and humility of true sense and taste and reality;
And from all the harms and hindrances of offensive manners and self-
        assertion:
Save us and help us, O Lord.

From affectation and untruth, conscious or unconscious,
from pretense and hypocricy,
from impulsive self-adaptation to the moment to please others or make
        circumstances easy:
    Strengthen us to true simplicity;
And from all false appearances:
Save us and help us, O Lord.

From love of flattery, from over-ready belief in praise,
from dislike of criticism,
and from the comfort of self-deception
        in persuading ourselves that others think better of us than we are:
Save us and help us, O Lord.

From all love of display and sacrifice to popularity,
from thinking of ourselves and forgetting you in our worship:
    Hold our minds in spiritual reverence;
And from self-glorification in all our words and works:
Save us and help us, O Lord.

From pride and self-will,
from the desire to have our own way in all things,
from overweening love of our own ideas and blindness to the value of
        others,
from resentment against opposition and contempt for the claims of others:
    Enlarge the generosity of our hearts and enlighten the fairness of
        our judgments;

And from all selfish arbitrariness of temper:
Save us and help us, O Lord.

From jealousy, whether of equals or superiors,
from grudging others success,
from impatience of submission and eagerness for authority:
    Give us the spirit of fellowship to share loyally with our co-workers in all
        true proportion;
And from all insubordination to just law and proper authority:
Save us and help us, O Lord.

From all hasty utterances of impatience,
from the retort of irritation and the taunt of sarcasm,
from all infirmity of temper in provoking or being provoked,
and from all idle words that may do hurt:
Save us and help us, O Lord.

In all times of temptatin to follow pleasure,
    to leave duty for amusement,
    to indulge in distraction, dissipation,
    dishonesty, or debt,
    or to degrade our high calling and forget our solemn vows;
And in all times of frailty in our flesh:
Save us and help us, O Lord.

In all times of ignorance and perplexity as to what is right and best
    to do:
    Direct us with wisdom to judge aright,
        and order our ways
        and overrule our circumstances
        by your good Providence;
And in our mistakes and misunderstandings:
Save us and help us, O Lord.

In times of doubts and questionings,
    when our belief is perplexed by new learning,
    and our faith is strained by doctrines and mysteries beyond
        our understanding:
    Give us the faithfulness of learners,
    and the courage of believers in your truth;
And alike from stubborn rejection of new revelations
and from hasty assurance that we are wiser than our forebears:
Save us and help us, O Lord.

From strife, partisanship, and division,
from magnifying our certainties to condemn all differences,
from building our systems to exclude all challenges,

and from all arrogance in our dealings with others:
Save us and help us, O Lord.

Give us knowledge of ourselves:
    our power and weaknesses, our spirit,
    our sympathy,
    our imagination, our knowledge, our truth:
Teach us by the standard of your Word,
    by the judgments of others,
    by examinations of ourselves;
Give us an earnest desire to strengthen ourselves continually
    by study, by diligence, by prayer and meditation;
And from all fancies, delusions, and prejudices
    of habit, or temper, or society:
Save us and help us, O Lord.

Give us true knowledge of others,
    in their difference from us and in their likeness to us,
that we may deal with their real selves –
    measuring their feelings by our own,
    but patiently considering their varied lives
    and thoughts and circumstances;
And in all our dealings with them,
from false judgments of our own,
from misplaced trust and distrust,
from misplaced giving and refusing,
from misplaced praise and rebuke,
Save us and help us, O Lord.

Chiefly we pray that we may know you and see you in all your works,
    always feel your presence near,
    hear you and know your call:
    Let your Spirit be our will, your Word our word;
And in all our shortcomings and infirmities,
may we have sure faith in your mercy.
Save us and help us, O Lord.

Finally, we pray, blot out our past transgressions,
heal the evils of our past negligences and ignorances,
and help us to amend our past mistakes and misunderstandings:
    Uplift our hearts to new love,
        new energy, new devotion,
        that we may be unburdened
        from the grief and shame of past unfaithfulness,
        and go forth in your strength
        to persevere through success and failure,

through good report and evil report,
even to the end;
And in all time of our tribulation,
and in all time of our prosperity:
Save us and help us, O Lord.

Here may follow the Lord's Prayer, if it is not used elsewhere in this service, and the Grace.

BISHOP GEORGE RIDDING

•149 A Litany of Farewell

Good Christian people, I bid you now pray for the saving presence of our living Lord

In this world:
He is risen.

In this Church:
He is risen.

In this community:
He is risen.

In this parish:
He is risen.

In the hearts of all faithful people:
He is risen.

But especially I bid you pray and give thanks now for _____ who is *(are)* leaving our community.

For expectations not met:
Lord, have mercy.

For grievances not resolved:
Lord, have mercy.

For wounds not healed:
Lord, have mercy.

For anger not dissolved:
Lord, have mercy.

For gifts not given:
Lord, have mercy.

For promises not kept:
Lord, have mercy.

And, also, for this portion of your lifelong pilgrimage which you have made with these people in this place:
Thanks be to God.

For friendships made, celebrations enjoyed, and for moments of nurture:
Thanks be to God.

For wounds healed, expectations met, gifts given, promises kept:
Thanks be to God.

For bread and wine, body and blood:
Thanks be to God.

For all the thoughtful, little kindnesses done to make the day better for someone:
Thanks be to God.

And so, to establish a home in another place with other members of the family of Christ:
Go in peace.

To continue the journey with new friends and new adventures, new gifts to give and to receive:
Go in peace.

To offer wisdom and experience, competence and compassion, in the vocation to which you are called:
Go in peace.

With whatever fears, whatever sadness, whatever excitement may be yours,
Go in peace.

With our faith in you, our hope for you, and our love of you:
Go in peace.

Here the People may add their own petitions.

The Lord watch between us while we are absent one from another – in the Name of the Father, and of the Son, and of the Holy Spirit.
Go in peace. Amen.

HENRY L. H. MYERS

Notes

Wherever an asterisk (*) occurs at the end of a particular litany, further information about that litany is given below. The various litanies are designated by their respective numbers which appear to the left of the page. All of the hymn tunes suggested here may be found in the *Lutheran Book of Worship* (1978); all but two of the tunes are also in the (Episcopal) *Hymnal 1940*.

1. The Great Litany, skillfully adapted from traditional material, first appeared in 1544. It was the work of Thomas Cranmer, principal architect of the first *Book of Common Prayer* (1549). This litany was the first official service to be prepared in the English language and was meant to be sung in procession.

If sung in this way today, the ministers and choir or the whole congregation may participate in the procession. Section I is sung in place and then the procession circles the inside or the exterior of the church while Sections II – V are sung. The final Section (VI) follows when all have returned to their original places. Music for the Great Litany may be obtained from the Church Hymnal Corporation, 800 Second Avenue, New York, NY 10017 *(Music for Ministers and Congregation II)*.

2. This *Bidding Prayer* may be used as a pastoral prayer in regular worship, or it may be used on special occasions. Perhaps the most famous contemporary instance of such a prayer is that used each Christmas at the Festival of Nine Lessons and Carols in King's College Chapel in Cambridge, England.

5. This litany is an adaptation of the *Prayer for the Whole State of Christ's Church* which Cranmer prepared for the first *Book of Common Prayer* (1549). It is taken from the *Ceylon Liturgy* which was officially authorized in 1938 for use in the Anglican Diocese of Colombo in what is now Sri Lanka.

8. The *South African Liturgy 1975* contains four alternative forms of intercession. This particular litany was proposed for inclusion by the "Africanization Committee" of the Church of the Province of South Africa.

9. The *Iran Experimental Liturgy 1971* was prepared for use by both Persian-speaking and English-speaking Anglicans in Iran.

11. The Community of Taizé in France is a Protestant monastic community which in the years since the Second World War has fashioned forms of worship of great ecumenical significance. The community's times of prayer each day now bring together Roman Catholics and Eastern Orthodox Christians as well as Anglicans and a wide variety of Protestants. The Taizé litanies in this collection come from either the *Taizé Office* (English translation: 1966) or *Praise God: Common Prayer at Taizé* (English: 1975).

12. This version of the *Eighteen Benedictions* is taken from *Gates of Prayer*, a service-book prepared for use in the synagogues of American Reform Judaism. The prayer itself, "the most official and most representative prayer of Judaism," was known to Jesus and almost certainly recited by him in the synagogue. It was also influential in the shaping of communal prayer in the early centuries of the Christian era.

13. Pope Gelasius (d. 496) prescribed that this prayer should be sung everywhere throughout the Church. It is the form the *Kyrie* took in the Roman Mass at the end of the 5th century.

14. This *Prayer for All Needs* is part of the oldest Christian prayer known outside the New Testament. It comes from a letter written to the Christian community at Corinth in the year 96 A.D. by St. Clement, probably the third successor of St. Peter as Bishop of Rome. The prayer as a whole closely follows the shape and movement of the Jewish *Eighteen Benedictions*.

15. Two musical settings of this litany may be found in the *Lutheran Book of Worship* (pp. 148-151). The concluding prayer may be spoken or intoned.

16. The *Lutheran Book of Worship* also provides a musical setting for this litany (pp. 168-173).

17. Lancelot Andrewes (1555-1626) was successively Bishop of Chichester, Ely, and Winchester. He served as one of the translators of the *Authorized (King James) Version* of the Bible; also over the years he compiled a set of devotions for his personal use. These were posthumously published in 1648 under the title *Preces Privatae* (Private Prayers).

19. A musical setting of this litany may be found in *Laudamus*, the supplementary hymnal in use at Yale Divinity School (pp. 245-246).

20. Seven of the litanies in this book are taken from *Come, Lord Jesus*, the English version of *Prières Bibliques* by Lucien Deiss. The English edition contains musical settings for the antiphons or congregational responses in the various litanies.

21-22. Musical settings of these litanies may be found in *The Book of Canticles* published by the Church Hymnal Corporation (see the note on Litany 1). The specific references are C-25D and C-26D (Litany 21); C-25F and C-26F (Litany 22).

24. This litany draws on material published in two issues of *Models for Ministers I* (September 2, 1973, and July 21, 1974).

28. John Wesley first used a *Service for Such as would Enter into or Renew their Covenant with God* in August 1755. He later published it as a pamphlet in 1780. The form given here is drawn from the *Methodist Book of Offices 1936* which was prepared

for use by British Methodists The three sets of hymn stanzas may be sung to the following tunes: (1) *Hanover;* (2) *St. Magnus;* and (3) *Azmon.*

30. This litany, also known as the *Benedicite,* may be sung to settings found in *The Book of Canticles* (see note on Litanies 21-22). The specific references are C-116, C-117 and C-118. The canticle draws on the *Song of the Three Young Men,* one of the books in the Apocrypha.

31. This litany comes from *The Psalms: A New Translation* where it appears as Psalm 135. Musical settings for the entire Psalter in this translation have been composed by the French Jesuit, Père Joseph Gelineau; they are available in this country from G.I.A. Publications, Inc., Chicago.

32. Where reference is made to Union Theological Seminary, New York City, it means that the litany in question was used in a service of worship there during the time that the compiler of this collection served as Chaplain to the Seminary (1969-73).

33. The Rev. Martha Blacklock is Vicar of St. Clement's Episcopal Church in New York City. She has also ministered to the Mother Thunder Mission, pioneering in the preparation of non-sexist or inclusive-language services. This litany is her own composition and it allows for the free mention of other faithful Christian women down the ages.

34. The Doxology at the close of this litany is sung to the familiar tune *Old Hundredth.*

35. This litany was composed in Polish on the eve of the Second World War. "Mankind will not find peace unless it turns with confidence to the Mercy of God" (words of Christ revealed to Sister Faustina Kowalska of the Congregation of Our Lady of Mercy).

37. This litany was inspired by Psalm 96; it concludes with the words of the *Sanctus,* which is based on Isaiah 6:3.

38. Parts of Psalm 149 and 150 are combined here with F. Pratt Green's hymn, written in 1971. The hymn stanzas may be sung to the tune *Engelberg.*

39. The *Alternative Service Book 1980* is in use in the Church of England in conjunction with the *Book of Common Prayer* (1662). Unlike previous liturgical practice, each of the Ten Commandments is here combined with a positive injunction from the New Testament.

40. This litany, taken from the July 21, 1974, issue of *Models for Ministers I,* is a further wedding of the Ten Commandments with New Testament teachings.

41. This litany was composed for a liturgical notebook submitted in conjunction with a course, The Roots of Liturgy, at Yale Divinity School.

42. This litany is used especially during the Ten Days of Penitence which culminate in the Day of Atonement, the most solemn occasion in the Jewish liturgical calendar. Known as the "Ovinu Malkenu" (from the opening words of each line), it is regarded by many as the most moving of all the litanies of the Jewish year.

46. This litany could well be sung by two or more voices to the setting familiar to many because of its use with some of these same words in the musical *Godspell*. The congregation would sing the response after each stanza to the same setting. The original litany by T.B. Pollock can be found in the (Episcopal) *Hymnal 1940* as numbers 229-231.

49. *Models for Ministers I,* issue of June 8, 1975.

51. This litany also appears in David Silk's collection, *Prayers for Use at the Alternative Services.*

54. The Advent Antiphons were traditionally sung before and after the *Magnificat* at Vespers from December 17 to December 23 inclusive. Each of the Antiphons welcomes the coming Messiah under one of the many titles ascribed to him in Holy Scripture.

55. This may be sung to its now "proper" tune, *Veni Emmanuel.*

62. This is taken from an Ash Wednesday liturgy contained in the January 1977 issue of *Modern Liturgy* (Vol. 4, No. 1, pp. 8-9, 12); the liturgy first appeared in *Service Resources for Pastoral Ministry,* 1976, #1 (Copyright 1976, Paulist Press, New York, NY).

65. Traditionally ascribed to St. Ignatius Loyola, the final prayer in this litany (the *Anima Christi*) appears to be much older, dating back to at least the early 14th century.

67. This litany could well be said in procession outside the church building on Palm Sunday; additional questions and benedictions could be improvised, answered in each case with the congregational responses given here which could readily be repeated from memory.

68. *Modern Liturgy,* issue of March 1978 (Vol. 5, No. 2, p. 30). This journal now appears eight times a year.

69. The *Orationes Sollemnes (Solemn Prayers)* were almost certainly part of the Roman Mass by the middle of the 5th century, if not earlier. They were removed at the end of the 5th century by Pope Gelasius who substituted the litany which now bears his name (see Litany 13). However, they were retained as part of the liturgy for Good Friday. The periods of silent prayer are an important reminder of the priestly responsibility of the whole People of God to make intercession for the Church and for the world.

70. The use of several leaders placed in different sections of the congregation would increase the effectiveness of this litany and heighten the identification of the worshippers with those who had some part in Christ's Passion.

75. The *Improperia (Reproaches)* have been since the 12th century a fixed part of the Roman liturgy for Good Friday. Traditionally they have been chanted by two choirs during the Veneration of the Cross. Here they have been adapted in order to avoid any trace of anti-Semitism. In the presence of the Crucified Savior we reproach ourselves for our ingratitude in spite of all God's goodness to us. Even though the

text refers to events in the history of Israel, it is we ourselves who continue to prepare "a cross for our Savior."

76. This litany is based on a sermon preached on Good Friday 1981 by Abbot Jerome at St. John's Abbey in Collegeville, Minnesota.

77. This is meant to be sung in procession with the Cross leading the way; the tune *Crucifer* is admirably suited to the text.

81. This *Easter Hymn* is part of an Easter homily attributed to Hippolytus who also wrote a treatise on the Paschal feast.

83. The hymn stanzas may be sung to *In Babilone.*

84. This litany, led by the deacon, occurs at the beginning of *An Order for the Lord's Supper* which was authorized in 1962 for use in the Church of South India. This liturgy, first prepared in 1950, reflects the ecumenical character of the Church which brings into one fellowship Indian Christians who had previously been Anglicans, Congregationalists, Methodists or Presbyterians.

85. *Models for Ministers I,* issue of June 2, 1974.

90. The saints and holy men and women invoked in this litany are included for the most part in either the Roman Catholic *Litany of the Saints* or in the listing of Lesser Festivals and Commemorations in the *Lutheran Book of Worship.* Some additional names have been added to make this a genuinely ecumenical litany.

91. The Free Church of Berkeley, California, first used this litany on June 15, 1968 "in a solidarity event for the Berrigans." Clearly, additional saints may also be invoked to "stand here beside us."

95. This ancient Irish metrical litany is headed with the words, "Colum cille composed this." If this attribution is correct, it was composed by St. Columba who in the sixth century founded the Abbey of Iona and from there evangelized the mainland of Scotland. He died on June 9, 597.

96. This also appears in *A Book of Family Prayer* prepared by Gabe Huck. The Doxology may be sung to the tune *Pleading Savior.*

101. *Models for Ministers I,* issue of October 27, 1974.

115. To underline the ecumenical character of this litany and also of the context in which it is being used, it would be desirable to choose two representatives from different traditions to lead it.

118. This litany is from *The Book of Prayers for Church and Home* (Christian Education Press, Philadelphia, 1962). It is taken from "An Act of Intercession for the Whole Church of Christ," included in *A Suggested Use for Pentecost, Christian Unity Sunday,* prepared by the North American Provisional Committee of the World Council of Churches, undated, but about 1945; the final prayer is from the Liturgy of St. Mark.

119. The various thanksgivings could be spoken in each case by a representative of that particular branch of the Christian family.

128. The *Renewal of Baptismal Vows* is especially appropriate on Easter Day (or during the Easter Vigil), the Day of Pentecost, All Saints' Day (or the first Sunday in November), and the Feast of the Baptism of our Lord (the First Sunday after the Epiphany).

131. The prayer at the presentation of the money-offering comes from the *South African Liturgy 1975*. In the Roman Catholic celebration of the Mass this prayer is not used. The prayers for the bread and wine are said quietly by the celebrant when an offertory song is being sung. The celebrant may say these prayers in an audible voice if there is no offertory song. In this case the people may respond to each prayer by saying: "Blessed be God for ever."

134. A musical setting of this litany has been written by Joseph Roff and is available from G.I.A. Publications, Inc., Chicago. The second section of Litany 62 may also be used at the Breaking of the Bread.

135. This quaint litany of thanksgiving, to be used after receiving Christ in the Sacrament of Holy Communion, is preserved in the *Lambeth Codex 546*, p. 37.

140. *Models for Ministers I*, issue of October 13, 1974.

146. These words have traditionally been sung to *Veni, Creator Spiritus*.

Bibliography

The litanies in this collection were compiled from the following sources which are listed alphabetically in the form in which they appear at the end of each particular litany:

Acts of Devotion, compiled by F. W. Dwelly. S.P.C.K., London, 1928.

Lancelot Andrewes, Bishop of Winchester: *Preces Privatae;* selections from the translation by F.E. Brightman, M.A., edited, with an introduction, by A.E. Burn, D.D., Methuen and Co., London, 1908.

The Alternative Service Book 1980: Services authorized for use in the Church of England in conjunction with *The Book of Common Prayer* (1662). Cambridge University Press, William Clowes (Publishers) Ltd., and S.P.C.K., 1980.

W.H. Auden: *For the Time Being: A Christmas Oratorio.* Random House, New York, 1945.

The Authorized Daily Prayer Book, Revised Edition, prepared by Joseph H. Hertz, late Chief Rabbi of the British Empire. Bloch Publishing Co., New York, 1948 (5709).

John Baillie: *A Diary of Private Prayer.* Charles Scribner's Sons, New York, 1949.

William Barclay: *Epilogues and Prayers.* Abingdon Press, New York and Nashville, 1963.

William Barclay: *Prayers for Help and Healing.* Harper and Row, New York and Evanston, 1968.

William Barclay: *Prayers for the Christian Year.* Harper and Row, New York and Evanston, 1965.

The Rev. Martha Blacklock (Mother Thunder Mission), St. Clement's Episcopal Church, 423 West 46th Street, New York, NY 10036.

The Book of Catholic Worship (1966). The Liturgical Conference, 2900 Newton Street N.W., Washington, D.C. 20018.

The Book of Common Prayer (1928). The Church Pension Fund, New York.

The Book of Common Prayer (1979). The Church Hymnal Corporation and Seabury Press, New York.

A Book of Family Prayers, prepared by Gabe Huck. Seabury Press, New York, 1979.

The Book of Occasional Services. The Church Hymnal Corporation, New York, 1979.

The Book of Prayers for Church and Home, compiled by Howard Paine and Bard Thompson. The Christian Education Press, Philadelphia, 1962.

Walter Russell Bowie: *Lift Up Your Hearts,* Enlarged Edition. Abingdon Press, New York and Nashville, 1956.

Bread for the World, 6411 Chillum Place N.W., Washington, DC 20012.

Carl F. Burke: *Treat Me Cool, Lord.* Association Press, New York, 1968.

Robert W. Castle, Jr.: *Prayers from the Burned-Out City.* Sheed and Ward, New York, 1968.

Church of South India: *The Book of Common Worship.* Oxford University Press, London, 1963.

Contemporary Prayers for Public Worship, edited by Caryl Micklem. S.C.M. Press, Ltd., London, 1967.

The Covenant of Peace: A Liberation Prayer Book, compiled by John P. Brown and Richard L. York. Morehouse-Barlow Co., New York (now Wilton, Connecticut), 1971.

The Cuddesdon College Office Book, Revised Edition. Oxford University Press, London, 1961.

The Daily Office Revised (with other prayers and services), edited by Ronald C.D. Jasper on behalf of the Joint Liturgical Group. S.P.C.K., London, 1978.

Lucien Deiss: *Come, Lord Jesus* (French original: *Prières Bibliques).* World Library Publications, Inc., 5040 North Ravenswood, Chicago, IL 60640.

Devotional Services for Public Worship, compiled by John Hunter. J.M. Dent, Ltd., London, 1903.

Early Christian Prayers (French original: *Prières des Premiers Chrétiens),* edited by A. Hamman, O.F.M., translated by Walter Mitchell. Longmans, Green and Co., Ltd., London, 1961.

Ember Prayers: A Collection of Prayers for the Ministry of the Church, compiled by John Neale. S.P.C.K., London, 1965.

Harry Emerson Fosdick: *A Book of Public Prayers.* Harper and Bros., New York, 1959.

Further Anglican Liturgies (1968-1975), edited by Colin Buchanan. Grove Books, Bramcote, Nottingham, 1975.

Gates of Prayer: The New Union Prayer Book (Weekdays, Sabbaths and Festivals: Services and Prayers for Synagogue and Home). Central Conference of American Rabbis, New York, 1975 (5735).

Norman C. Habel: *Interrobang: A Bunch of Unanswered Prayers and Unlimited Shouts*. Fortress Press, Philadelphia, 1969.

Larry Hard: *Contemporary Altar Prayers (Volume 3)*. C.S.S. Publishing Co., Inc., Lima, Ohio, 1973.

Raymond Hockley: *Intercessions at Holy Communion on Themes for the Church's Year*. A.R. Mowbray and Co., Ltd., London and Oxford, 1980.

The Hymnal of the Protestant Episcopal Church in the United States of America – 1940. The Church Hymnal Corporation, New York, 1943.

Irish Litanies: text and translation, edited from the manuscribts by the Rev. Charles Plummer, M.A. Henry Bradshaw Society, Volume 62 (1924), printed by Harrison and Sons, Ltd., London, 1925.

The Kingdom, the Power and the Glory: Services of Praise and Prayer for Occasional Use in Churches (American Edition of *The Grey Book*). Oxford University Press, New York, 1933.

Kyrie Eleison: Two Hundred Litanies, compiled by Benjamin F. Musser. The Newman Bookshop, Westminster, Maryland, 1945.

Laudamus: Services and Songs of Praise, edited by Jeffery Rowthorn, Bruce Neswick and W. Thomas Jones. Yale Divinity School, 409 Prospect Street, New Haven, Connecticut 06510.

Liturgy, now published quarterly by The Liturgical Conference, 2900 Newton Street N.W., Washington, D.C. 20018.

The Liturgy in English, edited by Bernard Wigan. Oxford University Press, London, 1962.

The Lutheran Book of Worship. Augsburg Publishing House, Minneapolis, 1978.

The Methodist Book of Offices 1936. The Methodist Publishing House, Wimbledon, London, 1936.

Samuel H. Miller: *Prayers for Daily Use.* Harper and Bros., New York, NY, 1957.

Models for Ministers I. World Library Publications, Inc., 5040 North Ravenswood, Chicago, Illinois 60640.

Modern Anglican Liturgies (1958-1968), edited by Colin Buchanan. Oxford University Press, London, 1968.

Modern Liturgy, now published eight times a year by Resource Publications, 7291 Coronado Drive, San Jose, California 95129.

Monday's Ministries: The Ministry of the Laity, edited by Raymond Tiemeyer. Parish Life Press, Philadelphia, 1979.

The Office of Creative Ministries, Missouri Area, United Methodist Church, P.O. Box 733, Columbia, Missouri 65205.

Praise God: Common Prayer at Taizé (French original: *La Louange des Jours,* 1971), translated by Emily Chisholm. Oxford University Press, New York, 1977.

Praise Him! A Prayerbook for Today's Christian, edited by William G. Storey. Ave Maria Press, Notre Dame, Indiana, 1973.

Pray Like This: Materials for the Practice of Dynamic Group Prayer, compiled by William G. Storey. Fides Publishers, Inc., Notre Dame, Indiana, 1973.

Prayers and Other Resources for Public Worship, compiled by Horton Davies and Morris Slifer. Abingdon Press, Nashville, 1976.

Prayers for a New World, compiled and edited by John W. Suter. Charles Scribner's Sons, New York, 1964.

Prayers for Today's Church, edited by Dick Williams. Augsburg Publishing House, Minneapolis, 1977.

Prayers for Use at the Alternative Services, compiled and adapted by David Silk. A.R. Mowbray and Co. Ltd., London and Oxford, 1980.

Prayers in Community (Volume 1 of *Contemporary Prayer),* edited by Thierry Maertens and Marguerite De Bilde, translated by Jerome J. DuCharme. Fides Publishers, Inc., Notre Dame, Indiana, 1974.

Prayers of the Faithful (for Sundays and Solemnities of Cycles A, B and C). Pueblo Publishing Co., New York, 1977.

Prayers, Thanksgivings, Litanies: prepared by the Standing Liturgical Commission of the Episcopal Church *(Prayer Book Studies 25).* Church Hymnal Corporation, New York, 1973.

The Psalms: A New Translation, translated from the Hebrew and arranged for singing to the psalmody of Joseph Gelineau. Paulist Press, New York, 1965.

The Roman Missal, revised by decree of the Second Vatican Council and published by authority of Pope Paul VI; English translation prepared by the International Commission on English in the Liturgy. Catholic Book Publishing Co., New York, 1974.

Rural People at Worship, compiled by Edward K. Ziegler. Agricultural Missions, Inc., New York, 1943.

Scripture Services: 18 Bible Themes, edited for group use by John Gallen, S.J. The Liturgical Press, Collegeville, Minnesota, 1963.

Kay Smallzried: *Litanies for Living – Spilled Milk.* Oxford University Press, New York, 1964.

Sojourners, 1309 L Street N.W., Washington, D.C. 20005.

Michael Sopocko: *God is Mercy,* translated from the Polish by the Marian Fathers. Grail Publications, St. Meinrad, Indiana, 1955.

The Student Prayer Book, edited and written by a Haddam House committee under the chairmanship of John Oliver Nelson. Association Press, New York, 1953.

Table Prayers, compiled by Mildred Tengbom. Augsburg Publishing House, Minneapolis, 1977.

The Taizé Office (French original: *Office de Taizé,* 1963), translated by Anthony Brown. Faith Press, London, 1966.

Carl T. Uehling: *Prayers for Public Worship.* Fortress Press, Philadelphia, 1972.

John Wesley's Prayers, edited by Frederick C. Gill. Epworth Press, London, 1951.

Herbert B. West: *Stay with me, Lord – A Man's Prayers.* Seabury Press, New York, 1974.

With One Voice: Prayers from around the World, compiled by Robert M. Bartlett. Thomas Y. Crowell Co., New York, 1961.

Elmer N. Witt: *Help It All Make Sense, Lord.* Concordia Publishing House, St. Louis and London, 1972.

Elmer N. Witt: *Time to Pray: Daily Prayers for Youth.* Concordia Publishing House, St. Louis, undated (preface dated St. Luke's Day, 1959).

Worldview, published by the Council on Religion and International Affairs, 170 East 64th Street, New York, NY 10021.

The Worshipbook. Westminster Press, Philadelphia, 1970.

Worship for Today: Suggestions and Ideas, edited by Richard Jones. Epworth Press, London, 1968.

Worship Services for Special Occasions, compiled and edited by Norman L. Hersey. World Publishing Co., New York and Cleveland, 1970.

WESTMAR COLLEGE LIBRARY